Managing Workplace Personality Disorders

A Comprehensive Guide to Identifying and Handling Narcissistic, Borderline, and Other Difficult Employees While Building Psychological Safety

Charlize Kaname McLean

Copyright © 2025 by Charlize Kaname McLean

All rights reserved. No part of this publication may be reproduced, distributed, or transmitted in any form or by any means, including photocopying, recording, or other electronic or mechanical methods, without the prior written permission of the publisher, except in the case of brief quotations embodied in critical reviews and certain other noncommercial uses permitted by copyright law.

ISBN: 978-1-7642339-8-9
Isohan Publishing
First Edition: 2025

This book is intended for educational and informational purposes only. The content provided herein does not constitute professional medical, psychological, legal, or employment advice. Readers should consult with qualified professionals before making decisions regarding workplace management, employee relations, or mental health matters.

The information in this book is not intended to diagnose, treat, cure, or prevent any mental health condition, nor should it replace consultation with qualified healthcare providers, employment attorneys, or human resources professionals. Any application of the recommendations set forth in this book is at the reader's discretion and sole risk.

All case studies, examples, and scenarios presented in this book are fictional composites created for educational purposes. Any resemblance to actual persons, living or dead, or actual events is purely coincidental. While based on common workplace situations and clinical understanding of personality disorders, no specific individuals or organizations are being depicted.

Any names used in examples are fictional. References to Dr. Grayce Sills or any other professionals mentioned are for stylistic purposes only and do not imply endorsement, affiliation, or actual authorship by those individuals. All external sources and research cited are properly attributed in the reference sections.

Laws regarding workplace accommodation, discrimination, and employment practices vary by jurisdiction and change over time. Readers should consult with qualified legal counsel familiar with current local, state, and federal regulations before implementing any policies or procedures discussed in this book.

The author and publisher shall not be liable for any loss of profit or any other commercial damages, including but not limited to special, incidental, consequential, or other damages arising from the use or inability to use the information contained in this book.

Table of Contents

Chapter 1: The Hidden Crisis in Modern Workplaces 1

    1.1 The $292 Billion Problem: Economic Impact of Toxic Workplace Behaviors 1

    1.2 Prevalence and Statistics: Who's Affected and How Many ... 2

    1.3 The Spectrum: From Difficult Personalities to Clinical Disorders 4

    1.4 Why Traditional Management Approaches Fail 6

    1.5 The Dual Perspective: Managing Up, Down, and Sideways . 8

Chapter 2: Clinical Foundations: Understanding Personality Disorders 12

    2.1 The DSM-5-TR Framework and Cluster System 12

    2.2 Cluster A: The Odd and Eccentric (Paranoid, Schizoid, Schizotypal) 14

    2.3 Cluster B: The Dramatic and Emotional (NPD, BPD, ASPD, Histrionic) 17

    2.4 Cluster C: The Anxious and Fearful (Avoidant, Dependent, OCPD) 20

    2.5 Subclinical Presentations: When Traits Don't Meet Full Criteria 23

Chapter 3: Legal Landscape and Organizational Responsibilities 27

    3.1 ADA and Mental Health: Rights, Protections, and Limitations 27

    3.2 EEOC Guidelines and Compliance Requirements 30

    3.3 The Direct Threat Standard and Safety Considerations 32

    3.4 Privacy, Confidentiality, and Information Management 35

    3.5 Creating Legally Sound Policies and Procedures 37

Chapter 4: Early Warning Signs and Red Flags 42

4.1 Behavioral Red Flags by Personality Type 42
　　4.2 The Escalation Timeline From Quirks to Crisis 46
　　4.3 Environmental Triggers and Contextual Factors 48
　　4.4 Team Dynamics as Early Warning Systems 50
　　4.5 Self-Assessment Tools for Managers and Employees 52

Chapter 5: The Impact Cascade: How Personality Disorders Affect Organizations 56
　　5.1 Team Disruption Patterns by Disorder Type 56
　　5.2 Productivity Metrics and Performance Impact 60
　　5.3 The Contagion Effect: How Toxicity Spreads 61
　　5.4 Organizational Culture as Enabler or Protector 63
　　5.5 Case Studies: Success Stories and Cautionary Tales 66

Chapter 6: Communication and Feedback Strategies 71
　　6.1 The CALM Method for De-escalation 71
　　6.2 Feedback Strategies for Different Personality Types 73
　　6.3 Written vs. Verbal Communication Decisions 76
　　6.4 Managing Emotional Volatility and Splitting Behaviors 78
　　6.5 Documentation While Communicating 80

Chapter 7: Performance Management and Progressive Discipline 84
　　7.1 Setting Clear Expectations and Boundaries 84
　　7.2 The Progressive Discipline Framework 86
　　7.3 Accommodation Integration in Performance Plans 88
　　7.4 When Traditional Approaches Don't Work 90
　　7.5 Termination Considerations and Risk Management 92

Chapter 8: Building Support Systems and Team Resilience 96
　　8.1 Team Composition and Role Design 96

8.2 Creating Psychological Safety Despite Challenges 98

8.3 Peer Support and Mentoring Programs 100

8.4 Managing Team Dynamics Around Difficult Members 102

8.5 Recovery Strategies After Toxic Employee Departure 104

Chapter 9: Personal Boundaries and Self-Protection 108

9.1 The Art of Professional Boundaries 108

9.2 Recognizing and Responding to Manipulation 110

9.3 Documentation as Self-Protection....................................... 113

9.4 Building Your Support Network 115

9.5 When to Consider Legal Consultation 117

Chapter 10: Strategic Communication for Self-Preservation 122

10.1 The Gray Rock Method: When and How........................ 122

10.2 Email Strategies and Written Documentation 124

10.3 Managing Up with Difficult Bosses.................................. 126

10.4 Navigating Office Politics and Alliances 128

10.5 Exit Conversations and Reference Management 131

Chapter 11: The Stay-or-Go Decision Framework 135

11.1 The STOP Method for Decision Making 135

11.2 Financial and Career Planning Considerations 137

11.3 Building Your Exit Strategy 139

11.4 Protecting References and Reputation 141

11.5 Recovery and Moving Forward.. 143

Chapter 12: Hiring and Screening Best Practices 148

12.1 Legal Considerations in Personality Screening 148

12.2 Behavioral Interview Techniques...................................... 150

12.3 Reference Checking for Character 153

12.4 Probationary Period Management 155

12.5 Early Intervention During Onboarding 157

Chapter 13: Creating Psychologically Safe Workplaces 162

13.1 The Four Pillars of Psychological Safety 162

13.2 Leadership Development and Accountability 164

13.3 Policy Frameworks That Work 166

13.4 Measurement and Continuous Improvement 168

13.5 Technology Tools for Culture Management 170

Chapter 14: Crisis Management and Professional Resources 175

14.1 Recognizing Mental Health Emergencies 175

14.2 EAP Integration and Utilization 178

14.3 When to Involve Legal Counsel 180

14.4 Fitness for Duty Evaluations 182

14.5 Return-to-Work Planning 184

Chapter 15: Emerging Trends and Future Workplace Evolution 188

15.1 Remote Work and Virtual Toxicity 188

15.2 AI and Technology in Behavior Management 190

15.3 Generational Differences in Mental Health Approaches.. 192

15.4 The Post-Pandemic Workplace Mental Health Revolution 194

15.5 Building Antifragile Organizations 196

Appendix A: Quick Reference Guides 201

Personality Disorder Characteristics Cheat Sheet 201

Communication Strategies by Type 204

Legal Compliance Checklist 205

Documentation Templates 206
Appendix B: Assessment Tools and Worksheets 208
    Team Health Assessment 208
    Personal Stress and Impact Tracker 209
    Stay-or-Go Decision Matrix 210
    Boundary Setting Worksheet 211
    Manager's Observation Log 212
Appendix C: Resources and Professional Contacts 213
    National Mental Health Organizations 213
    Legal Resources 214
    Professional Associations 214
    Recommended Training Programs 215
    Crisis Hotlines and Emergency Resources 216
Appendix D: Sample Policies and Procedures 218
    Accommodation Request Process 218
    Progressive Discipline Policy Template 219
    Workplace Behavior Standards 220
    Crisis Response Procedures 221
    Return-to-Work Guidelines 222
Appendix E: Case Studies and Scenarios 224
    NPD in Leadership: A Tech Startup Story 224
    BPD in Healthcare: Managing Emotional Volatility 225
    OCPD in Finance: When Perfectionism Paralyzes 227
    ASPD in Sales: Ethics and Boundaries 229
    Team Recovery After Toxic Departure 231

Reference 235

Chapter 1: The Hidden Crisis in Modern Workplaces

Organizations worldwide face an invisible epidemic that costs billions annually and destroys careers, teams, and lives. This crisis doesn't announce itself with fanfare or warning signs posted on conference room doors. Instead, it operates in the shadows—through the colleague who undermines every project, the supervisor who creates chaos through impossible demands, or the team member whose emotional volatility keeps everyone walking on eggshells.

Personality disorders in the workplace represent one of the most underaddressed yet costly challenges facing modern organizations. Unlike other workplace issues that receive attention through training programs, policies, and resources, personality-related dysfunction often gets dismissed as "difficult personalities" or "interpersonal conflicts." This dismissal comes at an enormous price.

1.1 The $292 Billion Problem: Economic Impact of Toxic Workplace Behaviors

The financial toll of personality disorder-related workplace dysfunction extends far beyond what most executives realize. Research indicates that toxic workplace behaviors cost U.S. organizations approximately $292 billion annually—a figure that dwarfs many corporate budgets and national programs.

This staggering number encompasses multiple cost categories. **Direct costs** include increased healthcare utilization, higher workers' compensation claims, and elevated employee assistance program usage. When employees work with individuals who have untreated personality disorders, stress-related medical conditions spike dramatically. Heart disease, depression, anxiety disorders, and substance abuse all increase within teams exposed to consistent dysfunction.

Indirect costs prove even more devastating. Turnover rates in departments with personality-disordered individuals often reach 60-80% annually—compared to healthy department averages of 10-15%. Each replacement hire costs organizations between 50-200% of the departing employee's annual salary when you factor in recruitment, training, and productivity losses.

Consider Sarah, a talented marketing director at a mid-sized technology company. Her department consistently produced award-winning campaigns until the company hired Marcus as creative director. Marcus displayed classic narcissistic personality traits—grandiose self-perception, exploitation of others, and rage when challenged. Within eight months, seven of Sarah's nine team members had quit. The department's campaign output dropped 70%, and client satisfaction scores plummeted. The company spent $340,000 replacing staff and lost two major clients worth $2.8 million in annual revenue. Marcus remained unaware of his impact, blaming departures on "weak team members who couldn't handle high standards."

Productivity losses create another massive cost center. Teams working with personality-disordered individuals spend an estimated 25-40% of their time managing interpersonal conflicts, walking on eggshells, or recovering from emotional disruption rather than focusing on core responsibilities. In knowledge work environments, this translates to millions in lost innovation and delayed project delivery.

Legal costs compound the financial damage. Harassment lawsuits, wrongful termination claims, and discrimination complaints often stem from mismanaged personality disorder situations. Organizations spend an average of $75,000-$150,000 defending each claim, regardless of outcome. More damaging, these legal actions typically expose organizations to broader scrutiny and negative publicity.

1.2 Prevalence and Statistics: Who's Affected and How Many

The prevalence of personality disorders in workplace settings significantly exceeds general population rates. While community studies suggest 10-15% of adults meet criteria for at least one personality disorder, workplace concentrations often reach 20-30% in certain industries and roles.

This concentration occurs for several reasons. Some personality disorders drive individuals toward specific career paths where their traits initially appear advantageous. Narcissistic individuals gravitate toward leadership roles, sales positions, and public-facing careers where confidence and self-promotion are valued. Antisocial personality traits may provide short-term success in high-pressure, results-oriented environments before destructive patterns emerge.

Industry-specific patterns reveal interesting concentrations:

- **Healthcare**: Borderline personality disorder appears in approximately 8-12% of healthcare workers, compared to 2-6% in the general population. The helping profession attracts individuals seeking to heal their own emotional wounds, but untreated borderline traits can create havoc in high-stress medical environments.
- **Technology**: Narcissistic and antisocial personality traits appear elevated in tech startups and competitive technology companies. The "move fast and break things" culture can initially reward impulsivity and disregard for others that later proves destructive.
- **Finance**: Antisocial and narcissistic personality disorders appear in 15-20% of high-pressure financial roles. The competitive, money-focused environment attracts individuals comfortable exploiting others for personal gain.

Position-level differences also emerge clearly. Executive and senior management positions show higher concentrations of Cluster B personality disorders (narcissistic, borderline, antisocial, histrionic) than front-line positions. This pattern creates particular organizational risk since personality-disordered leaders affect entire departments or companies.

Take the case of Jennifer, CEO of a regional healthcare system. She exhibited classic borderline personality disorder patterns—intense relationships that alternated between idealization and devaluation, emotional instability, and frantic efforts to avoid abandonment. She would promote executives rapidly, lavish them with praise and resources, then suddenly demote or terminate them over minor disagreements. Her leadership team turnover reached 90% annually. Hospital performance metrics declined across all measures—patient satisfaction, employee engagement, financial performance, and quality indicators. The board eventually removed Jennifer, but not before $15 million in losses and accreditation threats.

Demographic patterns show some variation by personality disorder type. Borderline personality disorder affects women at roughly three times the rate of men in clinical populations, though workplace presentations may be more balanced due to masking behaviors in professional settings. Narcissistic personality disorder shows less gender variation but tends to appear more frequently in individuals from higher socioeconomic backgrounds who received inconsistent praise and criticism during development.

1.3 The Spectrum: From Difficult Personalities to Clinical Disorders

Understanding the spectrum from normal personality variation to clinical disorder helps organizations respond appropriately to different situations. This distinction proves crucial for legal compliance, intervention planning, and resource allocation.

Normal personality variation represents the broad range of temperaments, communication styles, and behavioral preferences that make individuals unique. Someone might be naturally introverted, detail-oriented, or emotionally expressive without meeting any criteria for personality pathology. These differences often create workplace friction but respond well to training, coaching, and team development interventions.

Personality traits represent consistent patterns of thinking, feeling, and behaving that are more rigid than normal variation but don't yet cause significant impairment. An individual might show narcissistic traits—seeking admiration, lacking empathy, having grandiose fantasies—without meeting full criteria for narcissistic personality disorder. These traits may create workplace challenges but often remain manageable through clear expectations and feedback.

Subclinical presentations occur when individuals meet some but not all criteria for a personality disorder diagnosis. They might show four criteria for borderline personality disorder when five are required for diagnosis, or display antisocial behaviors that started in adulthood rather than childhood. These presentations often prove as disruptive as full disorders but may receive less recognition or accommodation.

Clinical personality disorders represent pervasive patterns of inner experience and behavior that deviate markedly from cultural expectations, are pervasive and inflexible, have onset by early adulthood, are stable over time, and lead to distress or impairment. The key factors are pervasiveness (affecting multiple life areas), inflexibility (resistant to feedback or situational demands), and impairment (causing problems in relationships, work, or other functioning).

Consider David, a software engineer whose obsessive-compulsive personality traits initially made him a valuable team member. His attention to detail and high standards helped catch bugs and improve code quality. However, over time these traits rigidified into obsessive-compulsive personality disorder. He became unable to delegate, spent hours perfecting minor details while missing deadlines, and created conflict with colleagues who didn't meet his impossible standards. Projects stalled as David insisted on reviewing every line of code multiple times. His behavior crossed from helpful personality traits to impairing personality disorder.

Environmental amplification plays a significant role in how personality traits manifest. Stressful work environments, unclear expectations, poor leadership, and high-pressure deadlines can amplify personality traits into dysfunction. Conversely, well-structured environments with clear boundaries and supportive management can help individuals with personality traits function effectively.

Masking and compensation complicate workplace assessment. Many individuals with personality disorders develop sophisticated masking behaviors to hide their difficulties in professional settings. They may function well for months or years before stressors overwhelm their coping mechanisms and underlying patterns emerge. This delayed emergence often catches organizations unprepared.

1.4 Why Traditional Management Approaches Fail

Standard management techniques often backfire spectacularly with personality-disordered employees, leaving supervisors frustrated and situations worse than before intervention attempts. Understanding why these approaches fail helps explain the need for specialized strategies.

Performance improvement plans (PIPs) typically focus on specific behaviors and measurable outcomes. However, personality disorders involve pervasive patterns that affect thinking, emotions, and behavior across multiple domains. Asking someone with narcissistic personality disorder to "accept feedback more gracefully" or someone with borderline personality disorder to "maintain emotional stability" addresses symptoms rather than underlying patterns.

Progressive discipline systems assume individuals can learn from consequences and modify behavior accordingly. Personality disorders often involve limited insight, externalization of blame, and difficulty learning from negative outcomes. Traditional discipline may escalate conflicts rather than resolve them.

Training and coaching work well for skill deficits but prove less effective for personality-based issues. You can't train someone out of a personality disorder through a workshop on communication skills or emotional intelligence. The underlying patterns will persist despite surface-level knowledge acquisition.

Team building activities may temporarily improve dynamics but rarely address fundamental personality-based dysfunction. Worse, some activities can trigger personality disorder symptoms—group exercises may threaten individuals with paranoid traits, while collaborative activities may frustrate those with antisocial tendencies.

Increased supervision often backfires with personality disorders. Micromanagement may trigger abandonment fears in borderline individuals, narcissistic rage in narcissistic individuals, or oppositional behavior in antisocial individuals. The additional attention may actually reinforce problematic behaviors rather than reduce them.

Consider Michael, a sales manager with antisocial personality disorder who consistently manipulated expense reports and client information. His supervisor, Helen, tried standard interventions: documenting incidents, providing training on company policies, implementing closer oversight, and placing Michael on a performance improvement plan. Each intervention escalated Michael's deceptive behavior. He became more sophisticated in his manipulation, began undermining Helen's authority with senior management, and started recruiting allies by sharing confidential information. The situation deteriorated until Helen was transferred to another department and Michael was promoted to regional sales director.

Emotional appeals fail with many personality disorders. Appeals to empathy, team loyalty, or organizational mission may be meaningless to individuals who lack empathy or view relationships as purely transactional. These approaches can even signal weakness that personality-disordered individuals exploit.

Flexibility and accommodation can backfire when applied inappropriately. While some accommodations may be legally required and therapeutically helpful, excessive flexibility may enable dysfunction or create unfair situations for other employees.

1.5 The Dual Perspective: Managing Up, Down, and Sideways

Workplace personality disorders create challenges that flow in all directions through organizational hierarchies. The traditional focus on managing difficult subordinates misses the equally destructive impact of personality-disordered supervisors and peers.

Managing up with personality-disordered supervisors requires entirely different strategies than managing down. Employees cannot discipline their bosses, set formal consequences, or remove them from positions. Instead, they must protect themselves while finding ways to function within dysfunctional systems.

Rachel worked for Thomas, a director with narcissistic personality disorder who took credit for others' work, flew into rages when challenged, and made impossible demands. Rachel learned to document everything, copy other managers on important emails, and present ideas in ways that made Thomas feel he originated them. She built relationships with Thomas's supervisor and peers to create alternative information channels. Most importantly, she developed exit strategies and transferred to another department when Thomas's behavior escalated beyond manageable levels.

Managing across organizational levels presents unique challenges. Peer relationships lack formal power structures but often involve collaboration, resource sharing, and informal influence networks. Personality-disordered colleagues can disrupt these relationships through manipulation, competition, and boundary violations.

Managing down receives the most attention but still requires specialized approaches. Traditional management tools prove inadequate, and managers need training in recognizing personality disorder patterns, setting appropriate boundaries, and knowing when to seek professional assistance.

Systemic impacts ripple throughout organizations regardless of hierarchy level. A personality-disordered individual in any position can affect multiple teams, create liability risks, and damage organizational culture. The impact often extends far beyond immediate reporting relationships.

Consider Lisa, an HR specialist with borderline personality disorder who processed employee benefits and handled confidential information. Her emotional instability and relationship difficulties didn't directly affect subordinates (she had none) or supervisors (who rarely interacted with her daily). However, her patterns of splitting (seeing others as all good or all bad), emotional volatility, and boundary violations affected employees throughout the organization. She shared confidential information with favored employees, processed benefits inconsistently based on personal relationships, and created drama that disrupted multiple departments.

Legal and ethical considerations complicate multi-directional management. Organizations have responsibilities to protect all employees from harassment and discrimination, regardless of hierarchy level. However, they also have obligations to accommodate mental health conditions. Balancing these responsibilities requires sophisticated understanding of legal requirements and practical management strategies.

Cultural factors influence how personality disorder impacts manifest across organizational levels. Some cultures emphasize hierarchy and authority, making personality-disordered supervisors particularly destructive. Other cultures prioritize team harmony, making any personality disorder symptoms more disruptive.

Communication patterns must adapt to different organizational relationships. Formal documentation may be appropriate when managing down but counterproductive when managing up. Peer relationships may require informal problem-solving approaches that would be inappropriate with supervisors or subordinates.

Reflection on Human Complexity

Working with personality disorders in professional settings forces us to confront uncomfortable truths about human nature and organizational life. These conditions represent extreme variations of traits we all possess to some degree—the need for admiration, fear of abandonment, desire for control, or tendency toward emotional reactivity.

The workplace becomes a laboratory where these human complexities play out daily, affecting productivity, relationships, and individual well-being. Recognition of this reality doesn't mean accepting destructive behavior or abandoning accountability. Instead, it requires developing more sophisticated approaches that balance compassion with boundaries, understanding with consequences.

Organizations that ignore personality disorder impacts do so at their own peril. The costs—financial, human, and cultural—compound over time. However, those that develop appropriate recognition and response strategies often find their overall management capabilities strengthened. Learning to work effectively with personality disorders builds skills that benefit all employee relationships.

The journey ahead requires patience, education, and sometimes difficult decisions. But for organizations willing to address this hidden crisis, the potential benefits extend far beyond individual problem situations to create healthier, more productive workplace cultures for everyone.

Key Insights for Workplace Success:

- Personality disorders cost organizations $292 billion annually through turnover, productivity losses, and legal challenges
- Workplace concentrations of personality disorders often exceed general population rates by 50-100%
- Traditional management approaches frequently backfire and may escalate problematic behaviors
- Personality disorder impacts flow in all organizational directions—up, down, and sideways

- Early recognition and specialized intervention strategies can prevent minor issues from becoming major crises
- Legal compliance requires understanding the distinction between protected mental health conditions and disruptive behaviors

Chapter 2: Clinical Foundations: Understanding Personality Disorders

The human personality represents one of psychology's most fascinating yet challenging areas of study. Unlike depression or anxiety, which represent episodic conditions that come and go, personality disorders involve enduring patterns of thinking, feeling, and behaving that shape how individuals experience themselves and others across their entire adult lives.

For workplace professionals, understanding these clinical foundations provides the knowledge base necessary to recognize patterns, respond appropriately, and avoid common misconceptions that lead to ineffective interventions. This chapter builds the clinical literacy necessary for informed decision-making about personality disorder issues in professional settings.

2.1 The DSM-5-TR Framework and Cluster System

The Diagnostic and Statistical Manual of Mental Disorders, Fifth Edition, Text Revision (DSM-5-TR) provides the standard classification system for personality disorders used by mental health professionals worldwide. This system organizes ten personality disorders into three clusters based on shared characteristics, creating a framework that helps predict patterns and inform intervention strategies.

Cluster A (Odd/Eccentric) includes paranoid, schizoid, and schizotypal personality disorders. Individuals with these conditions often appear strange or eccentric to others and typically have difficulty forming close relationships. In workplace settings, they may seem aloof, suspicious, or socially awkward, but their behaviors usually don't create the dramatic interpersonal conflicts seen with other personality disorder types.

Cluster B (Dramatic/Emotional/Erratic) encompasses narcissistic, borderline, antisocial, and histrionic personality disorders. These conditions create the most workplace disruption through emotional volatility, interpersonal exploitation, and dramatic behaviors. Cluster B personalities often draw attention to themselves and create intense, unstable relationships that affect entire teams.

Cluster C (Anxious/Fearful) includes avoidant, dependent, and obsessive-compulsive personality disorders. These individuals often appear anxious or fearful and may seek excessive reassurance or control. While less dramatic than Cluster B disorders, they can significantly impact productivity and team dynamics through perfectionism, indecisiveness, or social withdrawal.

The **general criteria** for any personality disorder require:

1. Pervasive pattern of inner experience and behavior that deviates markedly from cultural expectations
2. Pattern manifested in two or more areas: cognition, affectivity, interpersonal functioning, or impulse control
3. Pattern is inflexible and pervasive across personal and social situations
4. Pattern leads to clinically significant distress or impairment
5. Pattern is stable and of long duration, with onset traced back at least to adolescence or early adulthood
6. Pattern is not better explained by another mental disorder, substance use, or medical condition

Consider Jennifer, a project manager whose perfectionist tendencies initially seemed like assets. She caught errors others missed, maintained detailed documentation, and met all deadlines. However, over several years, these traits intensified into obsessive-compulsive personality disorder. She began spending hours on minor details, refused to delegate because others "didn't do things right," and created conflicts with team members who couldn't meet her impossible standards. Projects stalled as Jennifer insisted on reviewing every document multiple times. Her patterns met all general criteria—they were pervasive (affecting all work relationships), inflexible (she couldn't adapt standards to situational needs), stable (consistent over years), and impairing (affecting team productivity and her own advancement).

Dimensional vs. categorical thinking represents an important shift in understanding personality disorders. Rather than viewing these as discrete categories people either have or don't have, current thinking recognizes personality disorders as existing on continua. Someone might show moderate narcissistic traits without meeting full criteria for narcissistic personality disorder, or display borderline features only under stress.

Cultural considerations play crucial roles in personality disorder assessment. Behaviors considered normal in one culture might appear pathological in another. The DSM-5-TR emphasizes the importance of considering cultural background when evaluating personality patterns. For instance, collectivist cultures may view behaviors as healthy interdependence that individualist cultures might see as dependent personality traits.

Comorbidity patterns show that personality disorders frequently co-occur with other mental health conditions and with each other. Depression, anxiety, substance use disorders, and eating disorders all appear at elevated rates in individuals with personality disorders. This comorbidity complicates workplace presentations and intervention planning.

2.2 Cluster A: The Odd and Eccentric (Paranoid, Schizoid, Schizotypal)

Cluster A personality disorders often fly under the radar in workplace settings because they don't create obvious interpersonal drama. However, they can significantly impact team dynamics, innovation, and organizational culture through social withdrawal, suspiciousness, and unconventional thinking patterns.

Paranoid Personality Disorder involves pervasive distrust and suspiciousness of others, with individuals interpreting benign actions as malevolent. In workplace settings, this manifests as:

- Suspecting colleagues or supervisors of exploitation, harm, or deception without justification
- Reluctance to confide in others due to fears that information will be used maliciously
- Reading hidden demeaning or threatening meanings into benign remarks
- Bearing grudges and being unforgiving of perceived insults or slights
- Quickly reacting with anger or counterattacks to perceived threats
- Recurring suspicions about partner's or colleague's faithfulness or trustworthiness

Marcus worked as a systems administrator who gradually developed paranoid beliefs about his colleagues and supervisors. He became convinced that IT staff were monitoring his computer usage to find reasons for termination. He stopped participating in team meetings, believing others were sharing information to undermine him. When colleagues made casual comments about system performance, Marcus interpreted them as personal attacks on his competence. He began creating elaborate backup systems and documentation to "protect himself" from false accusations. His productivity declined as he spent increasing time verifying others' actions and protecting against imagined threats.

Schizoid Personality Disorder involves detachment from social relationships and restricted emotional expression. Workplace presentations include:

- Preference for solitary work activities
- Little interest in social or sexual relationships with colleagues
- Limited pleasure in activities, including workplace social events
- Emotional coldness, detachment, or flattened affect
- Indifference to praise or criticism from supervisors or peers
- Choosing solitary activities and avoiding team collaborations

Sarah, a data analyst, exhibited classic schizoid patterns. She arrived precisely at 8 AM, worked quietly at her desk, took lunch alone, and left at 5 PM without socializing. She declined all invitations to team events, office parties, or informal gatherings. Her work quality was excellent, but she showed no emotional response to praise, promotions, or criticism. Colleagues initially tried to include her but eventually gave up. Sarah seemed content with this arrangement and showed no desire for workplace friendships or connections.

Schizotypal Personality Disorder involves acute discomfort in close relationships, cognitive or perceptual distortions, and behavioral eccentricities. Workplace manifestations include:

- Ideas of reference (believing neutral events have special meaning)
- Odd beliefs or magical thinking inconsistent with cultural norms
- Unusual perceptual experiences
- Odd thinking and speech patterns
- Suspiciousness or paranoid thoughts
- Inappropriate or constricted affect
- Behavior or appearance that seems odd or eccentric
- Lack of close friends or confidants other than family

David, a marketing coordinator, displayed schizotypal features that initially seemed like creativity but gradually became disruptive. He believed certain color combinations in presentations had mystical significance and could influence client decisions. He wore unusual clothing combinations and made odd comments about "feeling energies" in different conference rooms. His ideas were often creative but presented in ways that made colleagues uncomfortable. He had difficulty maintaining eye contact and spoke in a peculiar, overly elaborate style that clients found off-putting.

Workplace impact patterns for Cluster A disorders typically involve:

- **Reduced collaboration** due to social withdrawal or suspiciousness
- **Innovation challenges** from reluctance to share ideas or paranoid thinking
- **Team building difficulties** when individuals won't participate in group activities
- **Communication barriers** from odd speech patterns or emotional detachment
- **Trust issues** that prevent effective delegation or teamwork

Management strategies for Cluster A personalities require different approaches than other personality disorders:

- **Respect boundaries** and don't force social interaction
- **Provide clear, written expectations** to reduce paranoid misinterpretations
- **Allow independent work** when possible
- **Avoid taking withdrawal personally** or pressuring for greater involvement
- **Focus on work quality** rather than social integration
- **Document interactions** to prevent later disputes or misunderstandings

2.3 Cluster B: The Dramatic and Emotional (NPD, BPD, ASPD, Histrionic)

Cluster B personality disorders create the most workplace disruption through intense emotions, dramatic behaviors, and chaotic interpersonal relationships. These conditions demand the most management attention and create the highest organizational risks.

Narcissistic Personality Disorder (NPD) involves grandiose self-perception, need for admiration, and lack of empathy. Workplace presentations include:

- Grandiose sense of self-importance and achievements
- Preoccupation with fantasies of success, power, or brilliance
- Belief in being "special" and deserving of special treatment

- Need for constant admiration and praise
- Sense of entitlement to favorable treatment
- Exploitation of relationships for personal advantage
- Lack of empathy for colleagues' needs or feelings
- Arrogant behaviors and attitudes

Robert, a sales director, exemplified narcissistic patterns that initially appeared as confidence and ambition. He frequently talked about his "exceptional" abilities and past achievements, often exaggerating details. He expected special privileges like better parking spots, larger offices, and exemptions from company policies. He took credit for team successes but blamed others for failures. When colleagues received recognition, Robert would minimize their contributions or redirect attention to himself. He showed no empathy when team members faced personal difficulties and became enraged when anyone questioned his decisions or authority.

Borderline Personality Disorder (BPD) involves instability in relationships, self-image, emotions, and marked impulsivity. Workplace manifestations include:

- Frantic efforts to avoid real or imagined abandonment
- Unstable and intense interpersonal relationships alternating between idealization and devaluation
- Identity disturbance with markedly unstable self-image
- Impulsivity in potentially damaging areas
- Recurrent suicidal behavior, gestures, or threats
- Emotional instability with marked reactivity
- Chronic feelings of emptiness
- Inappropriate, intense anger or difficulty controlling anger
- Transient, stress-related paranoid thoughts or dissociative symptoms

Linda, an HR coordinator, displayed borderline patterns that created chaos throughout the organization. She formed intense relationships with favored colleagues, sharing personal information and seeking constant reassurance. However, these relationships would suddenly shift to bitter conflicts over minor disagreements. She would idealize new supervisors as "the best boss ever" then devalue them as "incompetent" weeks later. Her emotions fluctuated dramatically—she might arrive upbeat and enthusiastic then become tearful and angry by afternoon. She made impulsive decisions about employee benefits and policies, then reversed them based on her emotional state. Her anger outbursts became legendary, and colleagues learned to avoid her on "bad days."

Antisocial Personality Disorder (ASPD) involves disregard for and violation of others' rights. Workplace presentations include:

- Failure to conform to social norms and lawful behaviors
- Deceitfulness through repeated lying, aliases, or conning others
- Impulsivity or failure to plan ahead
- Irritability and aggressiveness
- Reckless disregard for safety of self or others
- Consistent irresponsibility in work or financial obligations
- Lack of remorse for hurting, mistreating, or stealing from others

Michael, a procurement manager, showed antisocial patterns that initially seemed like decisive leadership. He routinely lied to vendors and clients about delivery dates, capabilities, and costs. He manipulated expense reports and vendor relationships for personal benefit. He showed no remorse when his actions caused problems for colleagues or clients, instead blaming others for "not understanding business." He was charming and persuasive when it served his purposes but became hostile and intimidating when challenged. He violated company policies repeatedly, then used legal technicalities or political connections to avoid consequences.

Histrionic Personality Disorder involves excessive emotionality and attention-seeking. Workplace manifestations include:

- Being uncomfortable when not the center of attention
- Inappropriate sexually seductive or provocative behavior
- Rapidly shifting and shallow expression of emotions

- Using physical appearance to draw attention
- Impressionistic speech lacking detail
- Theatrical, exaggerated emotional expression
- High suggestibility and influence by others
- Considering relationships more intimate than they actually are

Patricia, a public relations coordinator, exhibited histrionic patterns that initially seemed like enthusiasm and charisma. She dressed provocatively and made inappropriate comments about colleagues' appearances. She dominated meetings with dramatic stories and emotional displays that derailed productive discussions. She treated casual workplace interactions as intimate friendships, sharing personal details and expecting similar disclosure from others. Her emotions shifted rapidly from excitement to despair to anger, often multiple times per day. She became upset when others received attention and would create dramatic situations to refocus attention on herself.

Cluster B workplace risks include:

- **Legal liability** from harassment, discrimination, or hostile work environment claims
- **Team disruption** through emotional volatility and interpersonal conflicts
- **Ethical violations** from exploitation, deception, or boundary violations
- **Safety concerns** from impulsive or reckless behaviors
- **Cultural damage** when dramatic behaviors become normalized or create fear

2.4 Cluster C: The Anxious and Fearful (Avoidant, Dependent, OCPD)

Cluster C personality disorders create workplace challenges through excessive anxiety, perfectionism, and dependency that can paralyze decision-making and innovation while creating different types of team dysfunction.

Avoidant Personality Disorder involves social inhibition, feelings of inadequacy, and hypersensitivity to criticism. Workplace presentations include:

- Avoidance of occupational activities involving interpersonal contact
- Reluctance to get involved unless certain of being liked
- Restraint in intimate relationships due to fear of shame or ridicule
- Preoccupation with criticism or rejection in social situations
- Inhibition in new situations due to feelings of inadequacy
- Self-view as socially inept, unappealing, or inferior
- Reluctance to take risks or engage in new activities due to potential embarrassment

James, a talented software developer, showed avoidant patterns that limited his career advancement. He avoided presentations, client meetings, and team leadership roles despite technical excellence. He declined promotions that required increased interpersonal interaction. In meetings, he rarely spoke unless directly asked, and even then gave minimal responses. He interpreted neutral feedback as criticism and became distressed by performance reviews, even positive ones. He wanted workplace friendships but feared rejection, so he remained socially isolated. His avoidance of visibility prevented recognition of his contributions.

Dependent Personality Disorder involves excessive need for care and submissive, clinging behavior. Workplace manifestations include:

- Difficulty making everyday decisions without excessive advice and reassurance
- Need for others to assume responsibility for major life areas
- Difficulty expressing disagreement due to fear of loss of support
- Difficulty initiating projects due to lack of self-confidence
- Going to excessive lengths to obtain nurturance and support
- Feelings of helplessness when alone
- Urgently seeking new relationships when close ones end

- Unrealistic fears of being left to care for oneself

Susan, an administrative assistant, displayed dependent patterns that created problems for her supervisor and colleagues. She sought approval for routine decisions that fell within her authority. She couldn't prioritize tasks without detailed guidance and became anxious when supervisors were unavailable. She agreed with everyone to avoid conflict, even when she had relevant expertise. She formed intense attachments to supervisors and became distressed during vacation periods or leadership changes. She volunteered for extra work to maintain relationships, then felt overwhelmed and resentful but couldn't express these feelings directly.

Obsessive-Compulsive Personality Disorder (OCPD) involves preoccupation with orderliness, perfectionism, and control. Workplace presentations include:

- Preoccupation with details, rules, lists, and organization to the point that major goals are lost
- Perfectionism that interferes with task completion
- Excessive devotion to work and productivity to exclusion of leisure and friendships
- Overly conscientious, scrupulous, and inflexible about morality, ethics, or values
- Inability to discard worn-out or worthless objects
- Reluctance to delegate or work with others unless they submit to exact ways of doing things
- Miserly spending style toward self and others
- Rigidity and stubbornness

Thomas, a project manager, exhibited OCPD patterns that paradoxically reduced his effectiveness despite good intentions. He created elaborate planning documents and procedures that delayed project starts by weeks. He spent hours perfecting minor details while missing major deadlines. He couldn't delegate effectively because others didn't meet his exacting standards. He insisted on reviewing every document and decision, creating bottlenecks. He worked excessive hours but accomplished less than colleagues because of his perfectionist approach. He became rigid about procedures even when flexibility would serve project goals better.

Cluster C management challenges include:

- **Decision paralysis** from excessive fear or perfectionism
- **Productivity loss** from avoidance or perfectionist delays
- **Innovation barriers** from fear of risk or criticism
- **Delegation difficulties** when individuals can't trust others or make decisions
- **Team dynamics** affected by dependency or social withdrawal

2.5 Subclinical Presentations: When Traits Don't Meet Full Criteria

Many workplace personality issues involve subclinical presentations—individuals who show significant personality disorder traits without meeting full diagnostic criteria. These presentations often prove as disruptive as diagnosable disorders but may receive less recognition or accommodation.

Threshold issues arise because personality disorders require meeting specific numbers of criteria (typically 5 out of 9). Someone meeting 4 criteria may function similarly to someone meeting 5, but only the latter receives a formal diagnosis. In workplace settings, both presentations may require similar management approaches.

Situational factors can push subclinical traits into clinical range during stressful periods. Job changes, personal life stressors, organizational restructuring, or increased responsibilities may overwhelm coping mechanisms and reveal underlying personality patterns. What appeared to be normal personality variation may suddenly become impairing dysfunction.

Masking and compensation allow many individuals with personality disorder traits to function well in structured environments. They may develop sophisticated strategies to hide difficulties, seek roles that accommodate their traits, or receive support from understanding colleagues. However, these compensatory mechanisms can fail under stress or changing circumstances.

Workplace enabling sometimes maintains subclinical presentations by providing external structure, predictability, and support that mask underlying vulnerabilities. Individuals may function well in their current roles but struggle with promotions, transfers, or organizational changes that remove these supports.

Consider Maria, a financial analyst who showed narcissistic traits including grandiose self-perception, need for admiration, and limited empathy. However, she met only 4 of the 9 criteria for narcissistic personality disorder. In her structured role with clear metrics and regular recognition, she functioned well. Her confidence seemed like an asset, and her self-promotion led to advancement. However, when promoted to management, her traits became problematic. She couldn't handle criticism from subordinates, took credit for others' work, and showed little empathy for struggling team members. The additional stress and interpersonal demands pushed her subclinical traits into clinical dysfunction.

Assessment complexity increases with subclinical presentations because standard diagnostic tools may not capture the nuanced impairment these individuals experience. Functional assessment becomes more important than symptom counting—how do the traits affect work performance, relationships, and organizational functioning?

Intervention planning for subclinical presentations often mirrors approaches for full disorders but may require different intensity or focus. Environmental modifications, coaching, and skill development may prove more effective than intensive therapeutic interventions.

Understanding the Human Condition

Personality disorders represent extreme variations of traits we all possess—the need for control, fear of rejection, desire for admiration, or tendency toward perfectionism. They remind us that personality exists on continua rather than discrete categories, and that cultural context shapes our interpretation of normal versus pathological behavior.

In workplace settings, this understanding promotes both compassion and realistic expectations. These conditions reflect longstanding patterns that developed over years or decades—they won't change quickly or easily. However, individuals with personality disorders can learn to manage their symptoms, develop coping strategies, and function effectively in appropriate environments.

The goal isn't to cure personality disorders in the workplace but to create conditions where both affected individuals and their colleagues can be productive and safe. This requires sophisticated understanding of how these conditions manifest, realistic expectations about change, and practical strategies for managing their impact on organizational functioning.

Recognition of personality disorder patterns provides the foundation for all other interventions. Without this clinical literacy, well-meaning efforts often backfire and situations deteriorate. With appropriate understanding, organizations can develop humane, effective approaches that balance individual needs with collective productivity and safety.

Essential Clinical Knowledge:

- Personality disorders involve pervasive, inflexible patterns that cause significant impairment across multiple life areas
- Cluster B disorders (narcissistic, borderline, antisocial, histrionic) create the most workplace disruption
- Subclinical presentations may be as disruptive as diagnosable disorders but receive less recognition
- Cultural factors significantly influence the interpretation of personality patterns
- Traditional management approaches often fail because they don't account for the inflexible nature of personality patterns

- Environmental factors can either amplify or reduce personality disorder symptoms

Chapter 3: Legal Landscape and Organizational Responsibilities

The intersection of personality disorders and employment law creates one of the most complex areas of workplace management. Organizations must balance multiple competing obligations: protecting employees with mental health conditions from discrimination while maintaining safe, productive work environments for all staff. This balancing act requires sophisticated understanding of legal requirements, practical limitations, and risk management strategies.

Employment law in this area continues developing as courts interpret existing statutes in new contexts and societal understanding of mental health advances. What seemed clear-cut a decade ago now involves nuanced analysis of accommodation requirements, safety standards, and discrimination protections. Organizations that fail to stay current with these developments face significant legal and financial risks.

3.1 ADA and Mental Health: Rights, Protections, and Limitations

The Americans with Disabilities Act (ADA) provides the primary legal framework for workplace mental health accommodations, including personality disorders. However, the application of ADA protections to personality disorders involves complex questions about what constitutes a disability, reasonable accommodation, and undue hardship.

Disability definition under the ADA requires a physical or mental impairment that substantially limits one or more major life activities. For personality disorders, this analysis becomes complicated because these conditions involve personality traits that exist on continua. Courts must determine whether specific personality patterns rise to the level of substantial limitation.

The **2008 ADA Amendments Act** broadened the definition of disability and instructed courts to interpret "substantially limits" generously. This expansion increased protections for individuals with mental health conditions, including some personality disorders. However, courts still require evidence that the condition significantly restricts major life activities such as working, thinking, concentrating, or interacting with others.

Major life activities relevant to personality disorders include:

- **Interacting with others**: Critical for most workplace functions and often impaired in personality disorders
- **Thinking and concentrating**: Affected by emotional volatility, paranoid thoughts, or obsessive patterns
- **Working**: May be limited by interpersonal difficulties, perfectionism, or emotional instability
- **Sleeping**: Often disrupted in borderline and other personality disorders
- **Caring for oneself**: May be impaired during personality disorder episodes

Consider the case of Patricia, an accountant with borderline personality disorder who filed an ADA claim after termination. She documented that her condition substantially limited her ability to interact with others and maintain stable employment. Medical records showed a pattern of intense, unstable relationships and emotional volatility that affected her work performance. The court found that her condition qualified as a disability under the ADA, requiring the employer to engage in the interactive accommodation process.

Qualification requirements mean that not all personality disorder presentations receive ADA protection. The condition must:

- Constitute a mental impairment
- Substantially limit major life activities
- Be documented by qualified medical professionals
- Not pose direct threats that cannot be eliminated through reasonable accommodation

Interactive process obligations require employers to engage in good faith discussions about potential accommodations once they become aware of a disability. This process must be individualized, considering the specific employee's condition, job requirements, and potential accommodations.

Reasonable accommodation examples for personality disorders might include:

- **Modified supervision**: More frequent check-ins for individuals with dependency needs or less criticism for those with rejection sensitivity
- **Environmental modifications**: Private offices for those with paranoid traits or reduced social interaction requirements
- **Schedule adjustments**: Flexible hours to accommodate therapy appointments or emotional regulation needs
- **Policy modifications**: Allowing breaks for emotional regulation or modified dress codes for those with appearance concerns
- **Training accommodations**: Written rather than verbal instructions for individuals with concentration difficulties

Undue hardship limitations protect employers from accommodation requests that would fundamentally alter the job or create excessive burden. For personality disorders, this often involves situations where interpersonal skills are essential job functions that cannot be modified.

Direct threat exception allows employers to exclude individuals whose mental health conditions pose significant safety risks that cannot be eliminated through reasonable accommodation. This exception requires individualized assessment based on current medical evidence, duration and severity of risk, probability of harm, and accommodation possibilities.

Robert, a security guard with antisocial personality disorder, posed direct threat concerns due to his history of aggressive behavior and disregard for safety protocols. Despite accommodation attempts including additional training and supervision, he continued engaging in reckless behaviors that endangered colleagues and the public. The employer successfully defended termination based on direct threat grounds, supported by medical documentation and specific behavioral incidents.

Documentation requirements for ADA claims require medical evidence from qualified professionals establishing:

- The existence of a mental impairment
- How the impairment substantially limits major life activities
- Specific accommodation needs
- Effectiveness of proposed accommodations
- Safety considerations

3.2 EEOC Guidelines and Compliance Requirements

The Equal Employment Opportunity Commission (EEOC) provides detailed guidance on mental health conditions in the workplace, including enforcement priorities and investigation procedures. Recent EEOC publications reflect increased focus on mental health discrimination and accommodation requirements.

Enforcement trends show growing EEOC attention to mental health cases. The commission has prioritized cases involving:

- Failure to provide reasonable accommodations for mental health conditions
- Harassment or hostile work environments related to mental health status
- Retaliation against employees who request mental health accommodations
- Automatic exclusions of individuals with mental health conditions from employment

Investigation process for mental health discrimination claims follows standard EEOC procedures but involves specialized considerations:

- **Medical record review** requiring expertise in mental health conditions
- **Workplace culture assessment** examining attitudes toward mental health
- **Accommodation analysis** evaluating the interactive process and alternatives considered
- **Safety assessment** reviewing legitimate business justifications for adverse actions

Best practices emerging from EEOC guidance include:

- **Training programs** for managers on mental health accommodation requirements
- **Clear policies** outlining accommodation procedures and anti-discrimination protections
- **Documentation systems** tracking accommodation requests and interactive process steps
- **Regular reviews** of policies and practices for potential discriminatory impact

Common violations identified in EEOC investigations include:

- **Automatic disqualification** based on mental health diagnosis without individualized assessment
- **Failure to engage** in the interactive accommodation process
- **Inappropriate medical inquiries** beyond what's necessary for accommodation analysis
- **Retaliation** against employees who disclose mental health conditions or request accommodations
- **Hostile environment** created through harassment or stigmatization of mental health conditions

The EEOC resolved a high-profile case involving a telecommunications company that automatically excluded applicants with histories of mental health treatment from customer service positions. The settlement included monetary damages, policy changes, and mandatory training on mental health discrimination.

This case established important precedent about individualized assessment requirements.

Preventive measures recommended by the EEOC include:

- **Policy development** covering mental health accommodations and anti-discrimination protections
- **Manager training** on recognizing accommodation needs and conducting interactive process discussions
- **Employee education** about rights, responsibilities, and available resources
- **Regular auditing** of practices for potential discriminatory patterns
- **Vendor relationships** with mental health professionals for consultation and assessment

Documentation standards require organizations to maintain records showing:

- Accommodation requests and responses
- Interactive process communications
- Medical documentation reviewed
- Safety assessments conducted
- Decisions made and rationale
- Follow-up and effectiveness evaluation

3.3 The Direct Threat Standard and Safety Considerations

The direct threat standard provides the primary exception to ADA accommodation requirements, allowing employers to exclude individuals whose mental health conditions pose significant safety risks. However, applying this standard to personality disorders requires careful analysis of actual versus perceived risks.

Legal framework for direct threat analysis requires employers to demonstrate:

- **Significant risk** of substantial harm to self or others

- **Individualized assessment** based on current medical evidence
- **Objective evaluation** rather than speculation or stereotypes
- **Reasonable medical judgment** about the nature and severity of risk
- **Consideration of accommodation** to eliminate or reduce risk

Four-factor test established by the Supreme Court in *Chevron U.S.A. v. Echazabal* requires analysis of:

1. **Duration of risk**: How long will the dangerous condition persist?
2. **Nature and severity**: What type of harm might occur and how serious?
3. **Likelihood of harm**: What's the probability that harm will actually occur?
4. **Imminence**: How soon might the harm occur?

Personality disorder applications of direct threat analysis focus on specific behavioral patterns rather than diagnostic labels:

- **Violence history**: Documented aggressive behavior toward colleagues or clients
- **Impulsivity patterns**: Reckless decision-making that creates safety hazards
- **Substance abuse**: Co-occurring addiction that impairs judgment
- **Reality distortion**: Paranoid or delusional thinking affecting behavior
- **Emotional volatility**: Unpredictable reactions that create workplace tension

Consider the case of David, a forklift operator with borderline personality disorder who experienced emotional outbursts during relationship conflicts. His supervisor documented several incidents where David's emotional volatility created safety concerns—leaving equipment unattended, driving recklessly when upset, and engaging in heated arguments that distracted other operators. The employer conducted individualized assessment including psychological evaluation, safety record review, and accommodation analysis. When accommodations failed to eliminate safety risks, termination was upheld under direct threat standards.

Common misconceptions about direct threat include:

- **Diagnostic assumptions**: Assuming personality disorder labels automatically create safety risks
- **Speculative concerns**: Basing decisions on hypothetical rather than documented risks
- **Stereotypical thinking**: Applying generalized fears about mental illness rather than individualized assessment
- **Accommodation avoidance**: Using safety concerns to avoid accommodation obligations

Accommodation requirements apply even in potential direct threat situations. Employers must consider whether reasonable accommodations could eliminate or reduce safety risks before using the direct threat exception.

Evidence standards for direct threat determinations require:

- **Medical documentation** from qualified professionals
- **Behavioral records** showing actual incidents or patterns
- **Job analysis** identifying safety-critical functions
- **Accommodation assessment** evaluating potential risk reduction measures
- **Regular review** as conditions or accommodations change

Risk management strategies help organizations navigate direct threat determinations:

- **Clear policies** defining safety requirements and assessment procedures
- **Training programs** for managers on recognizing and responding to safety concerns
- **Documentation systems** tracking behavioral incidents and safety assessments

- **Professional consultation** with occupational health specialists and attorneys
- **Regular monitoring** of accommodation effectiveness and safety outcomes
-

3.4 Privacy, Confidentiality, and Information Management

Managing mental health information in workplace settings requires balancing multiple legal and ethical obligations. Organizations must protect employee privacy while sharing necessary information for accommodation and safety purposes.

HIPAA limitations mean that employment-related medical information generally falls outside HIPAA protections. However, employers still have confidentiality obligations under the ADA and state privacy laws.

ADA confidentiality requirements mandate that medical information be:

- **Collected only when necessary** for accommodation or safety analysis
- **Stored separately** from personnel files in secure locations
- **Shared on need-to-know basis** with appropriate personnel only
- **Protected from disclosure** to unauthorized individuals
- **Maintained confidentially** throughout and after employment

Permissible disclosures under the ADA include sharing medical information with:

- **Supervisors and managers** regarding work restrictions and accommodations
- **First aid and safety personnel** for emergency response purposes

- **Government officials** investigating compliance with disability laws
- **Insurance companies** for coverage and claims purposes
- **Workers' compensation offices** for related claims

Lisa, an HR director, violated ADA confidentiality requirements by discussing an employee's borderline personality disorder diagnosis with multiple managers during a staff meeting. She shared details about the employee's therapy attendance and medication needs that weren't relevant to accommodation planning. The employee filed complaints with the EEOC and state civil rights agency, resulting in significant monetary settlement and required training for all management staff.

Information management systems must ensure:

- **Secure storage** in locked files or password-protected electronic systems
- **Access controls** limiting who can view medical information
- **Audit trails** tracking who accessed information and when
- **Retention policies** governing how long medical information is kept
- **Disposal procedures** for secure destruction of outdated medical records

Training requirements for personnel handling medical information should cover:

- **Legal obligations** under ADA and state privacy laws
- **Confidentiality procedures** for collecting, storing, and sharing information
- **Permissible disclosures** and need-to-know limitations
- **Security measures** to prevent unauthorized access
- **Incident response** for privacy breaches or violations

Common violations of medical privacy include:

- **Gossiping** about employee mental health conditions

- **Inappropriate questions** beyond accommodation needs
- **Excessive sharing** of medical details with unnecessary personnel
- **Inadequate security** for medical information storage
- **Retaliation** for privacy complaints or concerns

Best practices for medical information management include:

- **Written policies** governing medical information handling
- **Regular training** for managers and HR personnel
- **Secure systems** for information storage and access
- **Clear procedures** for information sharing decisions
- **Legal consultation** for complex privacy questions

3.5 Creating Legally Sound Policies and Procedures

Effective policies and procedures provide the foundation for legal compliance while creating clear expectations for managers, employees, and HR personnel. These documents must balance legal requirements with practical implementation needs.

Policy components should address:

- **Non-discrimination commitments** covering mental health conditions
- **Accommodation procedures** outlining request and interactive process steps
- **Confidentiality protections** for medical information
- **Safety standards** and direct threat assessment procedures
- **Complaint processes** for discrimination or accommodation concerns

Accommodation procedures should specify:

- **Request process**: How employees can request accommodations
- **Documentation requirements**: What medical information is needed

- **Interactive process**: Steps for accommodation discussions
- **Decision criteria**: Factors considered in accommodation analysis
- **Appeal process**: Options if accommodation requests are denied
- **Monitoring procedures**: Follow-up on accommodation effectiveness

Manager responsibilities should include:

- **Recognition**: Identifying potential accommodation needs
- **Response**: Initiating interactive process discussions
- **Documentation**: Recording accommodation conversations and decisions
- **Implementation**: Ensuring approved accommodations are provided
- **Monitoring**: Evaluating accommodation effectiveness
- **Reporting**: Notifying HR of accommodation-related issues

Robert, a manufacturing supervisor, received complaints from several employees about a colleague's disruptive behavior. The colleague had disclosed bipolar disorder and requested accommodation for mood-related absences. Robert followed company policy by documenting specific behavioral incidents, consulting with HR about accommodation options, and implementing approved modifications including flexible scheduling and modified workstation location. When behaviors continued affecting team safety, he initiated policy-required assessments that led to additional accommodations and improved outcomes.

Training programs should cover:

- **Legal requirements** under ADA and related laws
- **Company policies** and procedures
- **Practical skills** for accommodation discussions
- **Documentation requirements** and best practices
- **Case studies** and scenario-based learning
- **Resource identification** for consultation and support

Documentation standards should require:

- **Incident records** describing specific behaviors and impacts
- **Accommodation logs** tracking requests, discussions, and decisions
- **Medical summaries** from accommodation-related evaluations
- **Training records** showing manager and HR education
- **Audit documentation** reviewing policy compliance and effectiveness

Regular reviews of policies and procedures should assess:

- **Legal compliance** with current ADA interpretations
- **Practical effectiveness** in workplace situations
- **Training adequacy** for managers and HR staff
- **Documentation quality** for legal defense purposes
- **Outcome measurement** of accommodation success rates

Professional resources for policy development include:

- **Employment attorneys** specializing in disability law
- **HR consultants** with mental health expertise
- **Occupational health professionals** for medical consultation
- **Insurance representatives** for risk management guidance
- **Industry associations** providing policy templates and guidance

Walking the Tightrope

Managing personality disorders in the workplace requires organizations to walk a careful tightrope between competing legal and practical obligations. On one side lies the requirement to accommodate mental health conditions and prevent discrimination. On the other side rest obligations to maintain safe, productive work environments for all employees.

This balancing act becomes more complex as societal understanding of mental health advances and legal interpretations continue developing. What worked five years ago may not provide adequate protection today. Organizations must stay current with legal developments while building practical systems for day-to-day management.

The most successful organizations view legal compliance not as a burden but as a framework for creating psychologically safe workplaces that benefit everyone. They invest in training, policies, and systems that protect both individuals with mental health conditions and their colleagues. They recognize that good legal compliance often aligns with good business practices.

However, legal compliance alone isn't sufficient. Organizations must also address the human elements—the fear, misunderstanding, and stigma that often surround personality disorders. Building cultures that support both accommodation and accountability requires leadership commitment that goes beyond policy development.

The legal landscape will continue evolving as courts interpret existing laws in new contexts and legislatures consider new protections. Organizations that build flexible, learning-oriented approaches to mental health accommodation will be best positioned to adapt to these changes while maintaining their core missions and values.

Strategic Legal Framework:

- ADA protections apply to personality disorders that substantially limit major life activities, requiring individualized assessment and reasonable accommodation
- Direct threat standards allow exclusion only when specific safety risks cannot be eliminated through accommodation
- Medical information confidentiality requirements extend beyond HIPAA to include ADA and state privacy protections
- EEOC enforcement priorities increasingly focus on mental health discrimination and accommodation failures
- Effective policies must balance legal compliance with practical implementation while providing clear guidance for managers

- Regular training and policy updates are essential as legal interpretations and societal understanding continue developing

Chapter 4: Early Warning Signs and Red Flags

The experienced nurse in the emergency department doesn't wait for a patient's blood pressure to reach stroke levels before taking action. She recognizes the subtle signs—the slight confusion, the asymmetric facial droop, the hesitation in speech—that signal trouble ahead. Similarly, managers and colleagues who understand personality disorder warning signs can intervene before workplace situations reach crisis proportions.

Personality disorders rarely announce themselves with dramatic fanfare on day one. Instead, they reveal themselves through patterns that develop over weeks and months—a colleague who seems charming but leaves a trail of damaged relationships, a supervisor whose perfectionism slowly transforms into paralyzing micromanagement, or a team member whose emotional reactions grow increasingly unpredictable. Learning to read these early signals protects both individuals and organizations from escalating dysfunction.

4.1 Behavioral Red Flags by Personality Type

Each personality disorder creates distinct behavioral signatures that alert observers can identify before situations become unmanageable. These patterns don't represent isolated incidents but consistent themes that persist across different situations and relationships.

Narcissistic Personality Disorder warning signs often appear as excessive confidence that crosses into grandiosity. Early indicators include taking credit for collaborative work, name-dropping important connections without genuine relationships, and consistently steering conversations toward personal achievements. More subtle signs include inability to tolerate criticism without defensive reactions, lack of genuine interest in others' experiences, and expectations of special treatment based on perceived superiority.

Marcus, a newly hired marketing director, initially impressed colleagues with his confidence and ambitious ideas. However, within three months, concerning patterns emerged. He routinely interrupted others in meetings to share tangentially related stories about his past successes. He submitted team proposals under his name alone, minimizing others' contributions. When his supervisor suggested minor revisions to a campaign, Marcus responded with a lengthy email detailing his superior qualifications and questioning the supervisor's understanding of modern marketing. Colleagues noticed he showed no curiosity about their backgrounds or ideas, treating conversations as opportunities for self-promotion rather than exchange.

Borderline Personality Disorder red flags typically involve emotional intensity that seems disproportionate to circumstances. Early warning signs include rapid relationship cycles where new colleagues are quickly idealized as "the best boss ever" or "an amazing teammate," followed by equally rapid devaluation over minor disappointments. Look for emotional volatility that creates workplace drama, frantic efforts to prevent perceived abandonment (such as excessive email checking or panic over routine schedule changes), and unstable self-image reflected in frequent career direction changes.

Sarah, an HR coordinator, displayed borderline patterns that initially seemed like enthusiasm and dedication. She formed intense friendships with new hires, spending hours after work helping them adjust and sharing personal details about her own struggles. However, these relationships inevitably soured. A colleague who was "absolutely wonderful" became "totally backstabbing" after declining a weekend social invitation. Sarah's emotions swung dramatically—arriving at work excited and energetic, then becoming tearful and angry by afternoon over minor interactions. She frequently expressed fears about job security despite positive performance reviews, seeking constant reassurance from supervisors.

Antisocial Personality Disorder warning signs center on disregard for rules and others' rights, though these patterns may be subtle initially. Early indicators include chronic lateness or absence without appropriate concern, taking credit or resources that belong to others, and showing charm that feels calculated rather than genuine. Look for patterns of bending truth when convenient, lack of remorse for mistakes that affect others, and willingness to break rules when unlikely to face consequences.

David, a sales representative, demonstrated antisocial patterns that colleagues initially attributed to "aggressive sales tactics." He consistently submitted inflated expense reports, claiming personal meals as client entertainment. He promised delivery dates he knew were impossible, then blamed manufacturing delays when clients complained. He showed remarkable charm with potential customers but treated support staff dismissively. Colleagues noticed he never accepted responsibility for lost sales, always finding external factors or other people to blame. He violated company social media policies by posting confidential client information but showed no concern when confronted.

Histrionic Personality Disorder red flags involve attention-seeking behaviors that disrupt workplace focus. Early warning signs include dramatic storytelling that seems designed to shock or impress, inappropriate emotional displays during routine work situations, and discomfort when not the center of attention. Look for overly familiar behavior with new colleagues, dress or appearance choices that seem calculated to draw attention, and tendency to perceive relationships as more intimate than they actually are.

Lisa, a public relations specialist, exhibited histrionic patterns that colleagues initially found entertaining but gradually became disruptive. She dominated team meetings with dramatic stories about her personal life, complete with exaggerated emotional expressions. She dressed provocatively for client meetings and made inappropriate comments about male colleagues' appearances. She interpreted professional mentoring as close friendship, sharing intimate details about her relationships and expecting similar disclosure from others. When colleagues received media coverage or recognition, Lisa would create dramatic situations that redirected attention to herself.

Obsessive-Compulsive Personality Disorder warning signs involve perfectionism and control that interferes with efficiency and relationships. Early indicators include excessive attention to minor details at the expense of major objectives, reluctance to delegate because others "don't do things right," and rigid adherence to rules even when flexibility would be more appropriate. Look for hoarding of tasks or information, difficulty making decisions due to perfectionist standards, and discomfort with ambiguity or change.

Thomas, a project manager, showed OCPD patterns that initially seemed like thoroughness and high standards. He created detailed project plans with elaborate tracking systems that took longer to maintain than the actual work. He insisted on reviewing every document and decision, creating bottlenecks that delayed project completion. He worked excessive hours but accomplished less than colleagues because he couldn't stop perfecting minor details. He became visibly agitated when team members suggested shortcuts or alternative approaches, insisting there was only one correct way to complete tasks.

Paranoid Personality Disorder red flags center on suspicious thinking that affects workplace relationships. Early warning signs include questioning colleagues' motives without justification, reluctance to share information due to fears it will be used against them, and tendency to perceive neutral comments as personal attacks. Look for grudges held over minor incidents, hypervigilance about office politics, and isolation that stems from distrust rather than preference.

Robert, a systems analyst, demonstrated paranoid patterns that colleagues initially attributed to introversion. He became suspicious when IT implemented new monitoring software, believing it was specifically designed to track his activities. He interpreted routine feedback as personal criticism and began documenting interactions to "protect himself" from false accusations. He stopped participating in team lunches and social events, convinced colleagues were talking about him negatively. He questioned the motives behind every policy change or organizational announcement, seeing hidden agendas where none existed.

4.2 The Escalation Timeline From Quirks to Crisis

Personality disorders don't appear overnight in workplace settings. They follow predictable escalation patterns that allow for early intervention if observers recognize the progression from manageable quirks to serious dysfunction.

The Honeymoon Phase typically lasts one to six months in new positions or relationships. During this period, individuals with personality disorders often present their best selves, using charm, intelligence, or apparent competence to make positive impressions. However, careful observers may notice subtle inconsistencies—stories that don't quite match, reactions that seem slightly inappropriate, or relationship patterns that hint at underlying difficulties.

The Stress Response Phase emerges as workplace demands increase or situations become challenging. This phase, usually occurring between months three to twelve, reveals how individuals handle pressure, feedback, and conflict. Personality disorder traits become more apparent as coping mechanisms prove inadequate for workplace stressors. The charming colleague becomes manipulative under pressure, the perfectionist becomes paralyzed by decision-making, or the confident leader becomes rageful when challenged.

The Pattern Establishment Phase occurs when personality disorder traits become entrenched in workplace relationships and routines. This typically happens after the first year, when individuals have learned the organizational culture and established their place within it. During this phase, problematic patterns become normalized by colleagues who adapt their behavior to accommodate the dysfunction rather than addressing it directly.

The Crisis Phase represents the breakdown of compensatory mechanisms and workplace relationships. This may be triggered by organizational changes, personal stressors, or accumulated conflicts that overwhelm the individual's ability to maintain their professional facade. During crisis phases, personality disorder symptoms become obvious and disruptive, often requiring formal intervention.

Consider Jennifer's progression as executive assistant to the CEO. Initially, she seemed dedicated and detail-oriented, volunteering for extra projects and staying late to ensure perfection. However, stress responses emerged when the company grew rapidly. She became territorial about her role, questioning others' access to the CEO and creating elaborate procedures for routine tasks. By her second year, she had established patterns of controlling information flow, creating drama around minor scheduling conflicts, and expressing emotional volatility that colleagues learned to navigate carefully. The crisis phase hit during a major organizational restructuring when her fear of abandonment triggered frantic efforts to prove her indispensability, including undermining other staff and creating conflicts that required executive intervention.

Acceleration factors can compress these timelines significantly. High-stress environments, unclear expectations, poor leadership, and organizational chaos can push individuals through escalation phases rapidly. Conversely, **protective factors** such as clear boundaries, consistent leadership, supportive colleagues, and structured environments can slow progression and sometimes prevent crisis phases entirely.

Intervention windows exist throughout this timeline, with earlier intervention generally proving more effective. During the honeymoon phase, setting clear expectations and boundaries can prevent later problems. Stress response phases offer opportunities for coaching and support. Pattern establishment phases require more intensive interventions but still allow for behavior modification. Crisis phases often necessitate formal disciplinary action or professional evaluation.

Warning sign clusters help predict progression speed. Multiple red flags appearing simultaneously suggest rapid escalation, while isolated incidents may indicate slower progression or situational factors rather than personality disorders. The intensity and frequency of concerning behaviors provide additional clues about intervention urgency.

4.3 Environmental Triggers and Contextual Factors

Workplace environments significantly influence how personality disorder traits manifest and progress. Understanding these triggers allows organizations to modify conditions that exacerbate problems while building supports that promote stability.

Organizational stress triggers include unclear expectations, frequent leadership changes, resource constraints, competitive cultures, and ambiguous communication. These conditions challenge anyone but prove particularly difficult for individuals with personality disorders who often struggle with ambiguity, change, and interpersonal complexity.

Role-specific triggers vary by position type and requirements. Customer service roles that require emotional regulation may trigger borderline personality traits. Leadership positions may activate narcissistic patterns. Detail-oriented positions might exacerbate obsessive-compulsive traits. Sales roles requiring relationship building could challenge individuals with antisocial or paranoid tendencies.

Interpersonal triggers emerge from specific relationship dynamics and communication patterns. Criticism may trigger narcissistic rage, abandonment fears may activate borderline emotional volatility, and authority conflicts might provoke antisocial resistance. Understanding these patterns helps predict and prevent problematic interactions.

Seasonal and cyclical triggers affect some individuals predictably. Anniversary dates of traumatic events, holiday seasons, performance review periods, and budget cycles can intensify personality disorder symptoms. Organizations that track these patterns can provide additional support during vulnerable periods.

Michael, a finance manager with borderline personality disorder, experienced predictable deterioration during quarterly reporting periods. The increased pressure, longer hours, and intense scrutiny triggered his abandonment fears and emotional volatility. His supervisor learned to provide extra check-ins during these periods, arrange temporary support staff, and modify expectations for interpersonal interactions. This proactive approach prevented the emotional meltdowns that had previously disrupted entire departments during critical reporting deadlines.

Protective environmental factors can reduce personality disorder impact significantly. These include clear policies and procedures, consistent leadership, predictable routines, supportive team members, and structured communication processes. Organizations can intentionally create these conditions to support all employees while particularly benefiting those with personality vulnerabilities.

Team composition effects influence how personality disorders manifest. Diverse teams with strong communication skills often contain personality disorder impacts better than homogeneous groups or teams with existing dysfunction. However, teams with multiple personality-disordered individuals can create toxic dynamics that amplify everyone's difficulties.

Leadership style impacts prove particularly influential. Authoritarian leadership may trigger oppositional responses in antisocial individuals but provide structure that helps borderline individuals. Democratic leadership styles may frustrate narcissistic individuals who expect special treatment but work well for most personality types. Laissez-faire leadership often proves problematic for individuals needing external structure and boundaries.

Cultural factors within organizations shape how personality disorder traits are perceived and managed. Some cultures tolerate or even reward certain problematic behaviors (such as narcissistic grandiosity in competitive sales environments), while others quickly identify and address interpersonal difficulties. Organizations must balance cultural values with healthy workplace standards.

4.4 Team Dynamics as Early Warning Systems

Teams often recognize personality disorder patterns before individual managers or HR departments because they experience the daily interpersonal impacts. Learning to read team dynamics provides early warning systems for emerging problems.

Communication pattern changes offer the first clues about personality disorder impacts. Teams may develop elaborate systems for sharing information to avoid certain individuals, create formal documentation for interactions that should be routine, or establish code words and signals to manage difficult personalities. These adaptations signal underlying dysfunction that requires attention.

Productivity shift patterns emerge as teams redirect energy from core work to relationship management. Time spent in hallway conversations about "difficult" colleagues, extra meetings to clarify communications, or duplicated efforts to ensure quality despite problematic team members all indicate personality disorder impacts on team functioning.

Emotional climate indicators include increased tension during team interactions, careful monitoring of certain individuals' moods, and general anxiety about team dynamics. Teams may develop protective behaviors such as avoiding controversial topics, tiptoeing around sensitive individuals, or bracing for emotional outbursts.

Participation pattern changes show up as certain team members becoming silent during meetings, others dominating discussions inappropriately, or productive members disengaging from collaborative activities. These shifts often reflect adaptations to personality disorder impacts rather than individual preferences or capabilities.

The marketing team at a software company gradually adapted to accommodate Patricia's histrionic patterns without realizing the full extent of their behavioral changes. Team meetings that once lasted thirty minutes now required an hour because Patricia dominated discussions with dramatic stories. Colleagues learned to schedule important conversations when Patricia was out of the office. They developed signals to warn each other about Patricia's mood states and planned activities around her emotional cycles. The team's creative output declined significantly as energy focused on managing interpersonal dynamics rather than innovative thinking.

Alliance formation patterns reveal how teams cope with personality disorder members. Healthy teams maintain inclusive dynamics, but teams with personality-disordered members often develop factions. Some colleagues align with the problematic individual to avoid becoming targets, others form protective alliances against them, and a few attempt to maintain neutrality. These dynamics create additional stress and reduce team effectiveness.

Conflict resolution changes show how teams modify their normal processes to accommodate personality disorders. Simple disagreements may require elaborate mediation processes, minor feedback may need careful scripting to avoid emotional reactions, and routine problem-solving may stall due to interpersonal complications.

Support seeking behaviors increase as team members look for guidance about managing difficult colleagues. Increased requests for transfers, more frequent conversations with HR, elevated use of employee assistance programs, and informal consultation with other managers all suggest personality disorder impacts on team functioning.

Performance compensation patterns emerge as productive team members work harder to compensate for dysfunction created by personality-disordered colleagues. This compensation may mask problems temporarily but creates burnout and resentment that eventually surface in turnover or formal complaints.

4.5 Self-Assessment Tools for Managers and Employees

Effective personality disorder recognition requires structured approaches that go beyond general impressions or emotional reactions. Self-assessment tools help managers and employees systematically evaluate situations and plan appropriate responses.

Behavioral observation frameworks provide systematic methods for documenting concerning patterns. The STOP method helps observers evaluate Specific behaviors, Timing and frequency, Objective impacts, and Persistent patterns. This framework prevents emotional reactions from coloring observations while ensuring comprehensive documentation.

Manager assessment checklists cover key areas including interpersonal relationships, work performance, emotional regulation, and policy compliance. These tools help managers distinguish between isolated incidents and persistent patterns while identifying specific areas needing intervention. Regular use of assessment checklists creates documentation that supports personnel decisions and accommodations.

Employee self-protection assessments help individuals evaluate their own experiences and develop appropriate responses. These tools cover emotional impact, productivity effects, safety concerns, and available resources. Self-protection assessments guide decisions about accommodation requests, complaint filing, and career planning.

Team health indicators provide frameworks for evaluating overall team functioning and identifying personality disorder impacts. These assessments examine communication patterns, productivity measures, emotional climate, and support needs. Teams can use these tools proactively to address emerging problems before they become crises.

Karen, a department supervisor, used behavioral observation frameworks to document concerns about James, whose paranoid traits were affecting team dynamics. She recorded specific incidents including dates, behaviors, and impacts on other team members. This systematic documentation revealed patterns that weren't obvious from individual incidents—James's suspiciousness increased during stress periods, his isolation deepened after perceived slights, and his productivity declined when he focused on imagined threats. The documentation supported accommodation discussions with HR and provided clear guidance for intervention planning.

Risk assessment matrices help evaluate the severity and urgency of personality disorder impacts. These tools consider factors such as safety concerns, legal risks, productivity impacts, and team disruption to prioritize intervention efforts. Risk assessments guide resource allocation and help determine appropriate response levels.

Intervention readiness checklists help managers prepare for difficult conversations and formal actions. These tools ensure adequate documentation, legal compliance, resource availability, and support systems before addressing personality disorder issues. Preparation checklists reduce the likelihood of escalation and improve intervention outcomes.

Support resource inventories catalog available assistance for both managers and employees dealing with personality disorder impacts. These inventories include internal resources (HR, employee assistance programs, occupational health), external resources (legal consultation, mental health professionals), and informal supports (mentoring, peer consultation). Resource awareness improves response effectiveness and reduces isolation.

Progress monitoring tools track intervention effectiveness and guide ongoing management strategies. These tools measure behavioral changes, team functioning improvements, and individual adaptation over time. Progress monitoring helps determine when interventions are working and when adjustments are needed.

Professional consultation guides help managers and employees decide when to seek expert assistance. These guides outline warning signs that indicate needs for legal consultation, mental health evaluation, or specialized training. Professional consultation can prevent minor issues from becoming major problems while ensuring appropriate expertise guides intervention planning.

Patterns in the Shadows

Personality disorders operate like shadows in workplace settings—present and influential but often unrecognized until they grow large enough to block out the light entirely. The behavioral patterns discussed in this material don't represent isolated quirks or temporary stress responses but persistent themes that affect individuals, teams, and organizations over time.

Recognition alone doesn't solve personality disorder problems, but it provides the foundation for all effective interventions. Managers who can identify escalation patterns can intervene during stress response phases rather than waiting for crisis episodes. Teams that understand personality disorder impacts can develop protective strategies that maintain productivity while supporting all members. Employees who recognize warning signs can protect themselves and make informed decisions about their careers and well-being.

The tools and frameworks presented here require practice and refinement to become truly useful. Like any clinical skill, personality disorder recognition improves with experience, feedback, and ongoing education. Organizations that invest in building these capabilities often find their overall management effectiveness improved as leaders become more sophisticated about human behavior and team dynamics.

However, recognition must be balanced with compassion and appropriate boundaries. The goal isn't to diagnose colleagues or create hostile environments for individuals with mental health conditions. Instead, the objective is to understand behavioral patterns well enough to respond effectively while maintaining respect for human dignity and legal compliance.

The patterns revealed through systematic observation provide roadmaps for intervention rather than condemnation. They help predict which environmental modifications might be helpful, which communication approaches might be effective, and which boundaries might be necessary. This understanding serves everyone's interests—individuals with personality disorders, their colleagues, and the organizations that employ them all.

Essential Recognition Skills:

- Early warning signs appear months before crisis situations, providing intervention opportunities for prepared observers
- Each personality disorder type creates distinct behavioral signatures that alert managers can identify and respond to appropriately
- Environmental factors significantly influence how personality disorder traits manifest and progress in workplace settings
- Team dynamics often reveal personality disorder impacts before individual assessments, making collaborative observation valuable
- Systematic assessment tools improve recognition accuracy while providing documentation for personnel decisions and accommodations
- Recognition skills require ongoing development and practice to become truly effective in workplace applications

Chapter 5: The Impact Cascade: How Personality Disorders Affect Organizations

A single drop of water seems harmless until it starts a cascade that carves through solid rock over time. Similarly, one individual with an untreated personality disorder can create organizational damage that spreads far beyond their immediate role or department. This cascade effect explains why personality disorder impacts often seem disproportionate to the number of affected individuals—their influence ripples through teams, departments, and entire organizational cultures in ways that compound over months and years.

Understanding these cascade patterns helps organizations recognize why traditional problem-solving approaches often fail. You can't address personality disorder impacts by focusing solely on the primary individual. Instead, you must understand and interrupt the ripple effects that touch multiple people, processes, and performance measures throughout the organization.

5.1 Team Disruption Patterns by Disorder Type

Each personality disorder type creates distinct patterns of team disruption that follow predictable trajectories. Understanding these patterns helps organizations anticipate problems, implement preventive measures, and respond more effectively when issues arise.

Narcissistic personality disorder creates team disruption through domination and devaluation patterns. These individuals consume disproportionate amounts of team time and attention while contributing less collaborative value. Teams develop elaborate systems to manage narcissistic colleagues' need for admiration while protecting themselves from exploitation and blame-shifting.

The engineering team at a aerospace company experienced classic narcissistic disruption patterns when Marcus joined as senior engineer. Initially, his confidence and technical knowledge impressed colleagues. However, within six months, team dynamics shifted dramatically. Marcus dominated technical discussions, interrupting others and dismissing ideas that weren't his own. He took credit for collaborative solutions while blaming team members for any implementation problems. Team meetings became platforms for Marcus's self-promotion rather than productive problem-solving sessions. Colleagues stopped sharing innovative ideas because Marcus would appropriate them. The team's creative output declined 40% as members focused more on protecting their contributions than advancing projects. Two experienced engineers requested transfers, citing Marcus's impossible behavior and management's failure to address it.

Borderline personality disorder disrupts teams through emotional volatility and relationship instability. These patterns create constant interpersonal drama that exhausts team emotional resources and diverts attention from core work activities. Teams may develop protective behaviors that exclude the borderline individual from important activities to avoid triggering emotional outbursts.

Sarah's borderline patterns created chaos in the customer service department of a telecommunications company. Her intense relationships with colleagues followed predictable cycles—she would idealize new team members, seek constant interaction and validation, then shift to anger and accusations over minor disappointments. Her emotional volatility meant team members never knew if they would encounter enthusiastic Sarah or tearful, angry Sarah on any given day. The team developed early warning systems to predict her mood states and modified their behavior accordingly. Customer service quality suffered as team members spent time managing Sarah's emotions rather than serving clients. The department's customer satisfaction scores dropped 25% over eight months as Sarah's patterns affected everyone's ability to focus on client needs.

Antisocial personality disorder disrupts teams through exploitation and rule-breaking that creates ethical compromises and legal risks. These individuals manipulate team dynamics for personal advantage while showing no concern for colleagues' well-being or organizational values. Teams may become complicit in problematic behaviors or develop elaborate monitoring systems to protect themselves.

David's antisocial traits systematically corrupted the sales team at a medical device company. He manipulated client information to steal colleagues' prospects, falsified activity reports to inflate his performance metrics, and shared confidential information to gain personal advantages. Team members initially tried to work collaboratively with David, but gradually realized he exploited every interaction for personal benefit. The team developed protective behaviors including password-protecting client files, copying management on all communications, and double-checking information David provided. Trust within the team eroded as members wondered who else might be engaged in similar behaviors. Team performance declined despite individual efforts as energy went toward self-protection rather than collaborative sales activities.

Histrionic personality disorder disrupts teams through attention-seeking behaviors that derail productive activities. These individuals create drama and emotional displays that distract from work objectives while demanding inappropriate levels of personal attention from colleagues. Teams may develop careful management strategies around histrionic members' emotional needs.

Patricia's histrionic patterns transformed the marketing team at a consumer goods company into a therapy group rather than a professional work unit. She dominated team meetings with personal stories and emotional displays that had little relevance to marketing objectives. She interpreted professional feedback as personal attacks, responding with theatrical emotional outbursts that made colleagues uncomfortable providing necessary input. She created romantic drama with colleagues that forced others to take sides or avoid team social activities. The team's focus shifted from creative marketing campaigns to managing Patricia's emotional needs and interpersonal conflicts. Campaign development timelines increased 60% as team energy went toward relationship management rather than creative work.

Obsessive-compulsive personality disorder disrupts teams through perfectionism and control that paralyzes decision-making and prevents timely task completion. These individuals create bottlenecks in team processes while insisting on unnecessary detail and rigid adherence to procedures that may not serve project objectives.

Thomas's OCPD patterns gradually strangled productivity in the project management team at a construction company. His perfectionist standards meant no document was ever complete enough, no plan sufficiently detailed, and no timeline adequately researched. He created elaborate tracking systems that required more time to maintain than the actual project work. He couldn't delegate effectively because others didn't meet his impossible standards, so work backed up waiting for his review and approval. Team members became frustrated with constant delays and began working around Thomas whenever possible. Project timelines stretched 30-50% beyond reasonable estimates as Thomas's perfectionism prevented timely completion of even routine tasks.

Paranoid personality disorder disrupts teams through suspicion and distrust that prevents effective collaboration and information sharing. These individuals create toxic environments where colleagues feel constantly watched and judged while productive teamwork becomes impossible due to secrecy and defensiveness.

Robert's paranoid traits poisoned the IT department's collaborative culture at a financial services firm. He became convinced that colleagues were monitoring his work to find grounds for termination. He stopped participating in team knowledge-sharing sessions, believing others would steal his ideas or use information against him. He questioned every policy change and organizational announcement, seeing hidden threats where none existed. His suspicious behavior made colleagues uncomfortable and defensive. The team's traditional collaborative problem-solving approach broke down as Robert refused to share information or trust others' intentions. Technical projects stalled as Robert's isolation prevented the knowledge sharing necessary for complex implementations.

5.2 Productivity Metrics and Performance Impact

Personality disorders create measurable impacts on organizational productivity that extend far beyond the affected individual's direct output. These impacts appear in multiple metrics and often prove more significant than initially apparent because they affect both efficiency and effectiveness across teams and departments.

Direct productivity measures show declining output from individuals with personality disorders as their symptoms interfere with focus, decision-making, and task completion. However, these direct measures often underestimate total impact because they don't account for the energy and time other employees spend managing personality disorder effects.

Indirect productivity impacts prove more significant and harder to measure. These include time spent by colleagues managing difficult relationships, duplicated work to compensate for unreliable contributions, delayed decisions due to interpersonal conflicts, and reduced innovation due to dysfunctional team dynamics. Studies suggest that indirect productivity losses from personality disorders can be three to five times larger than direct losses.

Quality deterioration patterns emerge as teams focus more on managing interpersonal dynamics than maintaining work standards. Projects may meet basic requirements but lack the innovation and attention to detail that characterize high-performing teams. Customer service quality often declines as employee energy goes toward internal relationship management rather than external client focus.

The accounting department at a regional hospital system experienced measurable productivity decline after hiring Jennifer, whose borderline personality traits created ongoing interpersonal drama. Direct measures showed Jennifer's work output was 20% below department standards—she completed fewer patient billing cycles and made more errors requiring correction. However, indirect impacts proved much larger. Other department members spent an estimated 15-20% of their time managing Jennifer's emotional needs, mediating conflicts she created, and compensating for her inconsistent performance. Department overtime increased 35% as staff worked extra hours to complete tasks delayed by Jennifer's interpersonal disruptions. Patient billing accuracy declined 12% as department focus shifted from quality control to relationship management. The total productivity impact was estimated at $180,000 annually in a department with six employees.

Innovation and creativity impacts appear as teams become risk-averse and conflict-avoidant to prevent triggering personality disorder symptoms. Brainstorming sessions may become stilted, controversial ideas get suppressed, and breakthrough thinking suffers as teams focus on maintaining interpersonal peace rather than pushing creative boundaries.

Decision-making delays multiply throughout organizations as personality disorder impacts create bottlenecks in collaborative processes. Simple decisions may require elaborate consensus-building to avoid emotional reactions, routine changes may trigger disproportionate resistance, and strategic planning may stall due to interpersonal conflicts rather than business considerations.

Communication efficiency declines as teams develop elaborate systems to manage personality disorder impacts. Simple information sharing may require multiple channels to ensure accurate transmission, routine feedback may need careful scripting to avoid emotional explosions, and normal workplace communications may become formal and documented to protect against later disputes.

Resource allocation distortions occur as organizations redirect management time, HR attention, and financial resources toward personality disorder management rather than productive business activities. These resource shifts may be invisible on traditional budget reports but represent significant opportunity costs for organizational development and growth.

5.3 The Contagion Effect: How Toxicity Spreads

Toxic workplace behaviors create contagion effects that spread beyond their original source through multiple transmission mechanisms. Understanding these contagion patterns helps organizations recognize why personality disorder impacts often seem to grow over time and affect people who have minimal direct contact with the primary individual.

Emotional contagion represents the most immediate transmission mechanism. Emotions spread rapidly through teams and departments, particularly negative emotions like anger, anxiety, and despair. Individuals with personality disorders often operate at high emotional intensity, and their feelings influence colleagues' emotional states through unconscious mimicry and empathetic responses.

Behavioral modeling occurs as team members adapt their behavior to cope with personality disorder impacts. These adaptations may include becoming more aggressive to compete with narcissistic colleagues, developing paranoid thinking in response to antisocial manipulation, or adopting perfectionist standards to avoid criticism from obsessive-compulsive team members. Over time, these adapted behaviors become habitual and spread to other relationships and situations.

Norm erosion happens gradually as teams lower their standards to accommodate personality disorder behaviors. Acceptable conduct boundaries shift as problematic behaviors become normalized through repetition and organizational tolerance. Teams may begin accepting late deliverables, poor communication, or interpersonal conflicts as normal workplace conditions rather than problems requiring solutions.

The customer service department at a software company experienced classic contagion effects after hiring Michael, whose antisocial traits gradually corrupted team culture. Initially, other team members maintained professional standards while trying to work collaboratively with Michael. However, his pattern of taking credit for others' work, manipulating client information, and breaking rules when convenient gradually influenced team behavior. Some colleagues began hoarding information to protect themselves from Michael's exploitation. Others started exaggerating their own contributions to ensure recognition. A few team members began bending rules themselves, reasoning that "everyone else does it." Within eighteen months, the department's culture had shifted from collaborative and ethical to competitive and self-protective. Customer complaints increased 40% as team members focused more on protecting themselves than serving clients.

Stress transmission spreads through organizations as personality disorder impacts create chronic stress that affects multiple individuals' health, performance, and relationships. Stressed employees may become irritable with colleagues, less patient with clients, and more prone to mistakes that create additional problems throughout the organization.

Trust degradation occurs as personality disorder behaviors damage interpersonal relationships and organizational confidence. When team members can't trust certain colleagues, they may become generally more suspicious and defensive. This degraded trust affects all relationships, not just those involving the personality-disordered individual.

Communication deterioration spreads as teams develop protective communication patterns that become habitual across all interactions. Formal documentation may replace informal discussion, careful word choice may substitute for direct feedback, and defensive communication patterns may become standard operating procedures rather than responses to specific individuals.

Leadership credibility erosion happens when managers fail to address personality disorder impacts effectively. Team members may lose confidence in leadership's judgment, fairness, or competence when problematic behaviors continue unchecked. This credibility loss affects leaders' ability to manage all aspects of team performance, not just personality disorder issues.

5.4 Organizational Culture as Enabler or Protector

Organizational culture plays a decisive role in determining how personality disorders manifest and spread within workplace settings. Some cultures inadvertently enable or even reward personality disorder behaviors, while others provide protective factors that limit their impact and prevent contagion effects.

Enabling cultural factors include competitive environments that reward individual achievement over collaboration, unclear expectations that allow manipulation and exploitation, weak accountability systems that fail to address problematic behaviors consistently, and leadership styles that model or tolerate inappropriate interpersonal conduct.

High-pressure, results-oriented cultures may initially reward personality disorder traits that appear to drive performance. Narcissistic confidence may be mistaken for leadership potential, antisocial manipulation may be seen as aggressive sales tactics, and obsessive perfectionism may be valued in detail-oriented roles. However, these cultures often experience delayed recognition of personality disorder costs as short-term performance gains mask long-term relationship and ethical problems.

Hierarchical cultures with rigid power structures may enable personality disorders by providing clear targets for exploitation and limited accountability for interpersonal behavior. Individuals with antisocial or narcissistic traits may thrive in environments where authority insulates them from consequences while subordinates have limited recourse for problematic treatment.

Change-resistant cultures may enable obsessive-compulsive patterns by reinforcing rigid thinking and resistance to adaptive modifications. These environments may reward perfectionist paralysis over flexible problem-solving and support controlling behaviors that prevent innovation and growth.

The technology startup experienced classic enabling cultural patterns that allowed narcissistic and antisocial behaviors to flourish unchecked. The company's "move fast and break things" culture initially rewarded employees who showed confidence, took risks, and pushed boundaries. However, this culture also enabled individuals with personality disorders to exploit others, ignore ethical standards, and create interpersonal chaos without consequences. Leadership viewed aggressive behavior as entrepreneurial drive and dismissed interpersonal conflicts as inevitable friction in high-performing teams. The company's rapid growth disguised productivity losses and team dysfunction until major clients began complaining about service quality and experienced employees started leaving for more stable environments.

Protective cultural factors include clear behavioral expectations with consistent enforcement, collaborative rather than competitive team structures, strong communication systems that address conflicts promptly, and leadership modeling that demonstrates healthy interpersonal relationships and emotional regulation.

Psychologically safe cultures provide protection by creating environments where employees feel comfortable reporting problematic behaviors, seeking help for interpersonal difficulties, and setting appropriate boundaries without fear of retaliation. These cultures recognize personality disorder impacts early and respond systematically rather than allowing problems to escalate.

Values-driven cultures with explicit ethical standards and behavioral expectations provide frameworks for addressing personality disorder impacts before they damage team functioning. These cultures maintain clear boundaries about acceptable conduct while providing support for individuals struggling with mental health challenges.

Learning-oriented cultures that value feedback, growth, and adaptation help prevent personality disorder behaviors from becoming entrenched by encouraging self-reflection and behavior modification. These cultures support both individual development and team effectiveness through ongoing education and skill building.

Accountability-focused cultures that consistently address problematic behaviors regardless of individual performance or status provide strong protection against personality disorder impacts. These cultures maintain clear consequences for interpersonal misconduct while supporting appropriate accommodations for mental health conditions.

5.5 Case Studies: Success Stories and Cautionary Tales

Real-world examples illustrate how organizations can either successfully manage personality disorder impacts or allow them to create widespread damage. These case studies provide practical insights into effective and ineffective approaches while demonstrating the long-term consequences of different management strategies.

Success Story: Regional Healthcare System

Mercy Regional Medical Center successfully managed a complex personality disorder situation involving Dr. Patricia Williams, a talented emergency physician whose borderline personality traits were creating chaos in the emergency department. Initially, Patricia's emotional volatility and relationship instability caused significant staff turnover and patient care concerns.

The hospital's response included multiple coordinated interventions. HR worked with Patricia to develop accommodation plans including modified schedules that provided emotional regulation time, peer support systems that offered structured relationship guidance, and clear communication protocols that reduced interpersonal conflicts. The medical director implemented team-based care models that distributed decision-making responsibilities while maintaining Patricia's clinical autonomy. Staff received training on working with colleagues who have mental health conditions, focusing on boundary setting and professional communication strategies.

The hospital also modified environmental factors that triggered Patricia's symptoms. They provided a private space for emotional regulation breaks, adjusted scheduling to avoid her most difficult periods, and created structured feedback systems that reduced perceived criticism and abandonment fears. Leadership maintained consistent communication about expectations while providing support for Patricia's professional development.

Results showed significant improvement across multiple measures. Staff turnover in the emergency department decreased from 45% to 12% annually. Patient satisfaction scores improved 25% as staff relationships stabilized and focus returned to patient care. Patricia's clinical performance remained excellent while her interpersonal functioning improved through structured support and clear expectations. The hospital's investment in accommodation and environmental modification proved cost-effective compared to recruiting and training replacement physicians.

Cautionary Tale: Technology Consulting Firm

TechSolutions Consulting experienced devastating consequences from failing to address Marcus Chen's narcissistic personality disorder patterns effectively. Marcus was hired as senior consultant based on impressive credentials and confident interview performance. However, his grandiose self-perception, exploitation of colleagues, and lack of empathy gradually destroyed team functioning and client relationships.

Initial warning signs included Marcus taking credit for collaborative work, undermining colleagues' contributions in client meetings, and showing no concern for others' professional development. Management dismissed these behaviors as competitive drive and individual ambition. When team members complained about Marcus's conduct, leadership attributed conflicts to personality clashes rather than recognizing systematic exploitation patterns.

The situation escalated as Marcus's behaviors became more problematic. He began sharing confidential client information to gain personal advantages, manipulating project data to inflate his performance metrics, and creating conflicts with clients when they questioned his recommendations. Team productivity declined as colleagues focused more on protecting themselves from Marcus's exploitation than serving client needs.

The crisis phase emerged when three major clients terminated contracts citing poor team dynamics and unprofessional conduct. Internal investigation revealed Marcus had created hostile work environments that violated company policies and potentially exposed the firm to legal liability. Six experienced consultants left the company within four months, taking specialized knowledge and client relationships with them.

The total cost included lost revenue of $2.8 million from terminated contracts, recruitment and training expenses of $450,000 for replacement staff, legal fees of $125,000 for investigation and potential litigation, and immeasurable damage to company reputation and client relationships. The firm eventually terminated Marcus but only after his patterns had created irreversible damage to team culture and client trust.

Success Story: Manufacturing Company

Precision Manufacturing Corporation successfully addressed Robert Johnson's paranoid personality traits through environmental modifications and supportive management approaches. Robert was a skilled machinist whose suspicious thinking and distrust of colleagues were affecting team safety and productivity.

The company's intervention strategy focused on reducing triggers while building trust through consistent, transparent communication. They provided Robert with detailed written procedures for all interactions, clear explanations for policy changes and organizational decisions, and regular one-on-one meetings with his supervisor to address concerns before they escalated.

Environmental modifications included organizing Robert's workspace to reduce feelings of surveillance, providing written documentation for all feedback and instructions, and ensuring consistent treatment from all supervisors and colleagues. The company also implemented team-building activities that built relationships gradually without forcing intimate self-disclosure that made Robert uncomfortable.

Management training helped supervisors understand paranoid thinking patterns without excusing problematic behaviors. They learned to provide extra reassurance during periods of organizational change, maintain consistent communication patterns that built trust over time, and address Robert's concerns respectfully while maintaining appropriate boundaries.

Results demonstrated that environmental modifications could successfully manage personality disorder impacts when implemented consistently. Robert's productivity improved 15% as his anxiety about workplace threats decreased. Safety incidents in his department dropped to zero as his hypervigilance was channeled into appropriate safety monitoring rather than interpersonal suspicion. Team relationships improved as colleagues learned to work effectively with Robert's communication needs while he became more trusting of their intentions.

Reverberations Through Time

The cascade effects of personality disorders in workplace settings remind us that human behavior creates waves that extend far beyond their apparent source. Like geological formations shaped by water flow over centuries, organizational cultures and team dynamics bear the imprint of personality disorder impacts long after the primary individual has moved on.

Understanding these cascade patterns requires systems thinking that considers relationships, environmental factors, and cultural influences rather than focusing solely on individual behaviors. Organizations that recognize these broader impacts can develop more effective interventions while building resilience against future challenges.

The success stories presented here share common elements: early recognition of problems, systematic intervention approaches, environmental modifications that reduce triggers, and consistent leadership that maintains both support and accountability. These organizations viewed personality disorder impacts as complex challenges requiring thoughtful responses rather than simple problems with obvious solutions.

The cautionary tales demonstrate what happens when organizations ignore cascade effects or hope problems will resolve themselves. The costs—financial, human, and cultural—compound over time as dysfunction spreads through teams and departments. Recovery from these impacts often requires much more effort and resources than prevention would have demanded.

The choice facing organizations isn't just about how to manage individual employees with personality disorders. It's about what kind of workplace culture they want to create and maintain over time. The decisions made today about addressing personality disorder impacts will shape organizational functioning for years to come through the cascade effects they either interrupt or allow to continue.

Core Impact Understanding:

- Each personality disorder type creates distinct team disruption patterns that follow predictable trajectories
- Productivity impacts extend far beyond direct measures to include indirect effects on collaboration, innovation, and decision-making
- Contagion effects spread toxic behaviors and attitudes throughout organizations via emotional, behavioral, and cultural transmission
- Organizational culture either enables personality disorder impacts or provides protective factors that limit their spread
- Successful management requires systematic approaches that address environmental factors, not just individual behaviors
- Early intervention prevents cascade effects that become increasingly difficult and expensive to address over time

Chapter 6: Communication and Feedback Strategies

The emergency room physician knows that how you speak to a panicked patient can mean the difference between cooperation and chaos, healing and harm. The tone of voice, choice of words, and timing of information delivery all matter tremendously in high-stakes situations. Similarly, communicating with individuals who have personality disorders requires the same level of precision and skill—understanding that what you say and how you say it can either escalate or de-escalate workplace conflicts.

Traditional communication approaches often backfire spectacularly with personality-disordered individuals because they don't account for the unique cognitive and emotional patterns these conditions create. A direct feedback session that works well with most employees might trigger narcissistic rage, borderline abandonment fears, or paranoid suspicions. Learning disorder-specific communication strategies protects both the individual and the workplace while increasing the likelihood of positive outcomes.

6.1 The CALM Method for De-escalation

The CALM method provides a structured approach for managing emotionally charged interactions with personality-disordered individuals. This framework helps you stay grounded while providing the specific responses that different personality types need to feel safe and heard.

C - Center Yourself forms the foundation of effective de-escalation. Before attempting to manage someone else's emotional state, you must regulate your own. This means taking three deep breaths, consciously relaxing your shoulders, and reminding yourself that their reaction isn't about you personally. You cannot control their response, but you can control your own behavior and emotional state.

A - Acknowledge Their Experience validates the person's emotional reality without necessarily agreeing with their interpretation of events. This step proves particularly important for personality disorders because these individuals often feel misunderstood or dismissed. Acknowledgment statements include "I can see you're feeling frustrated," "This situation seems really difficult for you," or "I hear that this is causing you stress."

L - Listen Actively requires giving the person your full attention while they express their concerns. Active listening means maintaining eye contact, asking clarifying questions, and reflecting back what you've heard. For personality-disordered individuals, feeling heard often reduces emotional intensity more effectively than trying to solve problems immediately.

M - Move Forward Collaboratively involves working together to identify next steps or solutions. This stage requires patience because personality-disordered individuals may need more time to process information and feel safe enough to engage in problem-solving. Collaboration builds their sense of agency while reducing defensive reactions.

Consider how Sarah, an HR manager, used the CALM method with Marcus, whose narcissistic traits had created conflicts with his marketing team. When Marcus stormed into her office demanding the team be restructured because they "couldn't handle his innovative approaches," Sarah first centered herself (recognizing his grandiosity wasn't a personal attack on her). She acknowledged his experience ("It sounds like you're feeling frustrated with the team dynamics"). She listened actively as he detailed his perceived mistreatment, asking questions like "Help me understand what happened in yesterday's meeting." Finally, she moved forward collaboratively ("Let's look at some specific ways to improve communication with your colleagues") rather than dismissing his concerns or defending the team.

Adaptation by personality type requires modifying the CALM approach based on specific disorder characteristics:

For narcissistic individuals, acknowledgment must include recognition of their competence or contributions. Listening should focus on their perspective without challenging their self-perception directly. Moving forward requires framing solutions in ways that preserve their sense of importance.

For borderline individuals, acknowledgment must address their emotional intensity without minimizing their feelings. Listening should include reassurance about the relationship stability. Moving forward requires clear commitments about ongoing support and connection.

For antisocial individuals, acknowledgment should focus on practical concerns rather than emotional validation. Listening should be structured and time-limited to prevent manipulation. Moving forward requires clear consequences and benefits tied to specific behaviors.

For paranoid individuals, acknowledgment must include recognition of their concerns without validating unrealistic fears. Listening should be transparent and documented. Moving forward requires extra explanations and reassurances about intentions.

The CALM method failed when Janet, a department supervisor, tried to use it with Robert, whose paranoid traits made him suspicious of any attempt at emotional connection. When she acknowledged his concerns about the new computer monitoring system, he interpreted her empathy as manipulation ("You're just trying to get me to relax so I'll say something you can use against me"). However, the method worked when Janet modified her approach—she acknowledged his concerns factually ("I understand you have questions about the monitoring system"), listened without trying to build emotional rapport, and moved forward by providing written documentation about the system's actual capabilities and limitations.

6.2 Feedback Strategies for Different Personality Types

Providing feedback to personality-disordered individuals requires understanding how each disorder type processes criticism, praise, and information about performance. Standard feedback approaches can trigger defensive reactions that make situations worse rather than promoting positive change.

Narcissistic personality feedback strategies must navigate the individual's grandiose self-perception and hypersensitivity to criticism. Direct criticism often triggers narcissistic rage, while excessive praise reinforces unrealistic self-assessment. The key lies in providing feedback that acknowledges competence while addressing specific behavioral changes.

Start feedback sessions by recognizing genuine strengths or accomplishments. Frame areas for improvement as opportunities to enhance already strong performance rather than corrections of deficiencies. Use collaborative language that positions you as supporting their success rather than judging their performance. Avoid global statements about personality or character, focusing instead on specific behaviors and their impact.

Michael, an IT director, successfully provided feedback to Jennifer, whose narcissistic traits were creating team conflicts. Instead of saying "Your communication style is too aggressive," he said "I know you're passionate about project quality, and I'd like to discuss some ways to share your expertise that might help the team feel more included in the process." This approach acknowledged her competence while addressing the behavioral issue without triggering defensive reactions.

Borderline personality feedback strategies must account for emotional volatility and fears of abandonment or rejection. These individuals often interpret feedback as relationship threats, leading to intense emotional reactions that derail productive conversations. Success requires extra reassurance about relationship stability and clear communication about ongoing support.

Begin feedback sessions by explicitly stating your commitment to their success and your intention to maintain a positive working relationship. Break feedback into smaller sessions rather than covering multiple issues at once. Provide specific examples rather than general observations, and always end with clear next steps and follow-up plans. Be prepared for emotional reactions and have support resources available.

David, a customer service manager, learned to provide feedback to Lisa, whose borderline traits caused emotional outbursts during performance discussions. He started sessions by saying "I want to help you succeed here, and nothing we discuss today changes my commitment to supporting your growth." He addressed one issue per meeting, provided specific examples, and always scheduled follow-up sessions within a few days to demonstrate ongoing engagement. This approach reduced Lisa's abandonment fears and allowed productive discussions about performance improvements.

Antisocial personality feedback strategies require clear structure and explicit consequences because these individuals often lack internal motivation for behavior change. Traditional appeals to team harmony, company values, or ethical considerations prove ineffective because antisocial individuals don't share these motivations.

Focus feedback on specific behaviors and their direct consequences for the individual's own goals and interests. Provide clear expectations with explicit outcomes for meeting or failing to meet them. Document everything and follow through consistently on stated consequences. Avoid emotional appeals or attempts to build empathy, focusing instead on logical cause-and-effect relationships.

Karen, a sales director, successfully managed feedback with Thomas, whose antisocial traits included manipulating client information and undermining colleagues. She focused on specific behaviors ("Sharing confidential client data violates company policy and could result in termination") rather than trying to build team loyalty. She provided clear consequences ("Meeting your sales targets requires maintaining client trust, which depends on following confidentiality protocols") that connected his behavior to his own interests. This approach proved more effective than appeals to team cooperation or company values.

Histrionic personality feedback strategies must manage attention-seeking behaviors while providing genuine recognition and support. These individuals often interpret feedback sessions as opportunities for dramatic expression, which can derail productive conversations about performance improvement.

Structure feedback sessions carefully to maintain focus on work-related issues. Acknowledge their emotional expressions without getting pulled into dramatic narratives. Provide specific, concrete feedback rather than general observations that might trigger storytelling. Use written follow-up to ensure important information isn't lost in emotional processing.

Obsessive-compulsive personality feedback strategies require patience and detailed explanations because these individuals often have difficulty processing feedback that challenges their perfectionist standards. They may become defensive about their methods or paralyzed by suggestions for improvement.

Provide detailed explanations for feedback points, including specific examples and rationale. Allow time for questions and discussion rather than rushing through feedback items. Focus on effectiveness rather than efficiency when suggesting improvements. Acknowledge their attention to detail while addressing areas where perfectionism interferes with productivity.

6.3 Written vs. Verbal Communication Decisions

Choosing between written and verbal communication can significantly impact the effectiveness of interactions with personality-disordered individuals. Each disorder type responds differently to different communication formats, and the wrong choice can escalate conflicts or create misunderstandings.

Written communication advantages include providing permanent records, allowing careful word choice, reducing emotional reactivity, and giving recipients time to process information before responding. Written communication works particularly well for paranoid individuals who may misinterpret verbal tone or become suspicious of verbal agreements they can't verify later.

Verbal communication advantages include immediate clarification opportunities, relationship building through personal interaction, faster resolution of simple issues, and reduced formality that may feel less threatening. Verbal communication often works better for borderline individuals who need reassurance about relationship stability and emotional connection.

Hybrid approaches combine written and verbal elements to maximize advantages while minimizing risks. These might include verbal discussions followed by written summaries, written agendas for verbal meetings, or verbal conversations to explain written documents.

Robert, a human resources manager, developed hybrid approaches for different personality types in his department. For Marcus (narcissistic traits), he provided written performance feedback that acknowledged accomplishments while addressing areas for improvement, followed by verbal discussions that allowed Marcus to ask questions and feel heard. For Sarah (borderline traits), he held verbal meetings to provide emotional reassurance and relationship stability, then followed up with written summaries to ensure clarity and demonstrate ongoing commitment. For David (antisocial traits), he relied primarily on written communication with clear expectations and consequences, using brief verbal check-ins only for clarification of written directives.

Timing considerations affect communication effectiveness regardless of format. Some personality types require immediate feedback to prevent anxiety or rumination, while others need processing time before engaging in discussions. Understanding these patterns helps determine both format and timing for maximum effectiveness.

Documentation requirements often drive communication format decisions, particularly for performance management or disciplinary situations. However, documentation needs should be balanced against relationship maintenance and communication effectiveness to achieve both legal protection and positive outcomes.

6.4 Managing Emotional Volatility and Splitting Behaviors

Emotional volatility and splitting behaviors represent two of the most challenging communication issues when working with personality-disordered individuals. These patterns can derail workplace conversations, create interpersonal drama, and interfere with productive problem-solving.

Emotional volatility involves rapid, intense changes in emotional state that seem disproportionate to triggering events. This pattern appears most commonly in borderline personality disorder but can occur with other types as well. Managing volatility requires understanding triggers, recognizing escalation patterns, and implementing de-escalation strategies.

Common volatility triggers include perceived criticism or rejection, changes in routine or expectations, interpersonal conflicts, and stress from work demands. Learning to recognize these triggers allows proactive intervention before emotions escalate beyond manageable levels.

De-escalation strategies for emotional volatility include remaining calm yourself, acknowledging their emotional experience, avoiding logic-based arguments during emotional peaks, and redirecting focus to specific, actionable steps. Never dismiss or minimize intense emotions, as this typically intensifies rather than reduces emotional reactivity.

Jennifer, a department manager, learned to manage emotional volatility in Lisa, whose borderline traits caused workplace disruptions during stressful periods. When Lisa became tearful and angry during a project deadline discussion, Jennifer acknowledged her stress ("I can see this deadline is creating a lot of pressure for you") rather than minimizing her reaction. She waited for the emotional intensity to decrease before discussing practical solutions, and she provided reassurance about their working relationship ("We'll figure this out together, and I'm committed to supporting you through this project"). This approach reduced the frequency and intensity of Lisa's emotional outbursts over time.

Splitting behaviors involve seeing people as either completely good or completely bad, with rapid shifts between these extreme positions. Individuals with splitting tendencies may idealize colleagues one day and demonize them the next over minor interactions. This pattern creates workplace drama and makes consistent relationships nearly impossible.

Managing splitting behaviors requires maintaining consistent responses regardless of your current status in their perception. Don't get drawn into the drama of being idealized or demonized. Instead, maintain professional boundaries and consistent communication patterns that don't change based on their emotional reactions to you.

Preventing splitting escalation involves avoiding taking sides in interpersonal conflicts, refusing to participate in gossip or complaints about other colleagues, and maintaining neutrality when individuals try to recruit allies against perceived enemies. These behaviors often intensify splitting patterns by confirming the person's black-and-white thinking about relationships.

Mark, a team leader, successfully managed splitting behaviors from Robert, whose borderline traits caused him to alternate between praising and criticizing team members based on minor interactions. When Robert complained that "Sarah is completely incompetent and shouldn't be on this team," Mark responded with "I understand you're frustrated with yesterday's meeting outcome. Let's focus on specific ways to improve communication for the next project" rather than agreeing with or defending against the character assassination. This approach prevented the team division that splitting behaviors often create.

6.5 Documentation While Communicating

Effective documentation of interactions with personality-disordered individuals serves multiple purposes: legal protection, performance tracking, pattern recognition, and communication clarity. However, documentation must be balanced with relationship building and genuine communication to avoid creating defensive or paranoid reactions.

Documentation best practices include recording objective behaviors rather than subjective interpretations, noting specific dates and circumstances, including witness information when appropriate, and focusing on work-related impacts rather than personal characteristics. Good documentation tells a story that outside observers can understand and evaluate.

Timing of documentation matters significantly. Immediate documentation captures details accurately but may interfere with relationship building if done obviously during interactions. Delayed documentation risks losing important details but allows focus on the human interaction during conversations. Most effective approaches involve brief notes during meetings followed by detailed documentation shortly afterward.

Format considerations include whether to use formal incident reports, email summaries, meeting notes, or performance tracking systems. The format should match the purpose and audience while maintaining professional tone and objective language throughout.

Shared documentation involves sending summaries to the individual after meetings or conversations. This approach increases transparency, reduces misunderstandings, and demonstrates commitment to clear communication. However, shared documentation must be carefully worded to avoid triggering defensive reactions while maintaining accuracy.

Patricia, an HR director, developed effective documentation practices for managing several employees with personality disorder traits. After feedback sessions, she sent email summaries highlighting key discussion points, agreed-upon action steps, and follow-up timelines. This approach reduced later disputes about what was said while demonstrating her commitment to fair and transparent communication. Her documentation included specific behavioral examples ("During the team meeting on March 15, you interrupted colleagues three times and dismissed their suggestions without discussion") rather than general characterizations ("you're too aggressive in meetings").

Legal compliance considerations require documentation that could support personnel decisions while protecting both individual and organizational interests. This includes recording accommodation discussions, performance improvement efforts, and safety concerns that might affect employment decisions.

Privacy and confidentiality requirements limit how documentation can be shared and stored. Medical information about personality disorders must be kept separate from personnel files, and access must be limited to individuals with legitimate business needs.

Documentation pitfalls include over-documenting routine interactions (which can feel punitive), using judgmental language instead of objective descriptions, failing to document positive interactions and improvements, and creating documentation that could be seen as harassing or discriminatory.

Using documentation proactively involves sharing relevant information with supervisors, HR staff, and other managers who need to understand behavioral patterns for effective interaction. This sharing must be done carefully to protect privacy while ensuring consistent organizational responses to personality disorder challenges.

Communication with personality-disordered individuals reminds us that behind every difficult behavior lies a human being struggling with fundamental challenges in thinking, feeling, and relating to others. The strategies presented here aren't manipulation techniques designed to control people, but rather skills for building genuine connections that serve everyone's interests.

The most effective communicators learn to see past the surface behaviors to understand the underlying fears, needs, and motivations that drive personality disorder symptoms. They recognize that narcissistic grandiosity often masks deep insecurity, that borderline volatility reflects terror of abandonment, and that antisocial manipulation may be the only relationship skill the person has ever learned.

This understanding doesn't excuse problematic behaviors or eliminate the need for clear boundaries and consequences. Instead, it provides a foundation for communication approaches that address both the immediate situation and the underlying human needs that drive difficult behaviors.

The frameworks and strategies presented here require practice and patience to implement effectively. Like any clinical skill, they improve with experience and thoughtful reflection on what works and what doesn't in different situations. Organizations that invest in building these communication capabilities often find their overall workplace culture improves as managers and employees develop more sophisticated interpersonal skills.

Communication remains one of the most powerful tools available for managing personality disorder impacts in workplace settings. Used skillfully, these approaches can transform destructive patterns into productive relationships while maintaining the boundaries and expectations necessary for effective organizational functioning.

Core Communication Framework:

- The CALM method provides structured de-escalation approaches that can be adapted for different personality disorder types
- Feedback strategies must account for each disorder's unique sensitivities and processing patterns to avoid triggering defensive reactions
- Written versus verbal communication decisions significantly impact interaction effectiveness and should be chosen based on individual needs and circumstances
- Emotional volatility and splitting behaviors require specific management techniques that maintain stability while addressing underlying concerns
- Documentation serves multiple purposes but must be balanced with relationship building and privacy protection to remain effective
- Successful communication requires understanding the human fears and needs that drive personality disorder symptoms while maintaining appropriate boundaries

Chapter 7: Performance Management and Progressive Discipline

The seasoned airline pilot knows that when instruments show system failures, you don't ignore the warning lights or hope the problems fix themselves. You follow established procedures, make necessary adjustments, and sometimes ground the aircraft until repairs are completed. Performance management with personality-disordered employees requires the same systematic approach—clear procedures, consistent implementation, and recognition that some situations may require removing individuals from their roles to protect everyone's safety.

Traditional performance management assumes employees can learn from feedback, modify their behavior based on consequences, and respond to coaching with improved performance. These assumptions often prove false with personality disorders, where behavioral patterns are deeply ingrained and resistant to conventional interventions. Success requires modified approaches that account for the rigid thinking patterns, limited insight, and defensive reactions that characterize these conditions.

7.1 Setting Clear Expectations and Boundaries

Clear expectations and firm boundaries form the foundation of effective performance management with personality-disordered employees. These individuals often struggle with ambiguity, misinterpret social cues, and may exploit unclear policies for personal advantage. Precision in expectation-setting prevents many problems while providing solid ground for accountability measures.

Specificity requirements go far beyond typical job descriptions to include detailed behavioral expectations that most employees understand intuitively. Instead of expecting "professional communication," specify exactly what this means: "Respond to emails within 24 hours, use respectful language in all interactions, avoid interrupting colleagues during meetings, and address disagreements privately rather than in group settings."

Written documentation of expectations proves essential because personality-disordered individuals may later claim they weren't informed of requirements or misunderstood verbal instructions. Written expectations also protect managers from accusations of unfair treatment while providing clear standards for evaluation and accountability.

Behavioral boundaries must address specific patterns that personality disorders typically create. For narcissistic individuals, boundaries might include "Take turns speaking in meetings, acknowledge others' contributions before presenting your own ideas, and accept supervisor feedback without defensive arguments." For borderline individuals, boundaries could specify "Maintain professional demeanor during difficult conversations, schedule personal discussions for appropriate times, and avoid creating drama around routine workplace changes."

Marcus, a finance director, successfully managed Jennifer, whose borderline traits had previously created chaos in budget planning meetings. He established specific boundaries including "Express concerns about budget items during designated discussion periods, avoid personal comments about colleagues' proposals, limit emotional reactions to professional disagreements, and schedule individual meetings to discuss concerns that feel personal or overwhelming." These boundaries, provided in writing and reviewed monthly, helped Jennifer maintain professional behavior during high-stress budget seasons.

Consequence clarity removes ambiguity about what happens when boundaries are violated. Personality-disordered individuals often test limits and may exploit unclear consequences for continued problematic behavior. Clear consequence statements include "Violating confidentiality policies will result in written warning for first offense and termination for second offense" rather than vague threats about "disciplinary action."

Accommodation integration requires building reasonable accommodations into expectation-setting without compromising essential job functions. This might include modified communication methods for individuals with paranoid traits, structured feedback sessions for those with borderline patterns, or additional processing time for obsessive-compulsive individuals.

Regular review processes ensure expectations remain clear and relevant as situations change. Monthly or quarterly reviews provide opportunities to clarify expectations, address emerging issues, and modify boundaries based on actual workplace experiences. These reviews also demonstrate organizational commitment to fair treatment and continuous improvement.

The legal department at a consulting firm developed highly specific expectations for David, whose antisocial traits had created ethical concerns and client relationship problems. Their written expectations included detailed guidelines about client confidentiality, expense reporting procedures, time tracking requirements, and interpersonal conduct standards. Each expectation included specific examples of acceptable and unacceptable behaviors, clear measurement criteria, and explicit consequences for violations. This approach prevented the manipulation and boundary-testing that had previously characterized David's employment pattern.

Cultural considerations affect how expectations should be communicated and enforced. Some organizational cultures emphasize flexibility and trust, while others rely on formal procedures and clear hierarchies. Expectations must align with organizational culture while providing the structure that personality-disordered individuals need for successful functioning.

7.2 The Progressive Discipline Framework

Progressive discipline with personality-disordered employees requires modifications to standard approaches because these individuals often don't respond to traditional learning models. Their conditions involve rigid thinking patterns, limited self-awareness, and defensive reactions that can make conventional discipline ineffective or even counterproductive.

Modified progression steps account for personality disorder characteristics while maintaining fair treatment standards. Traditional progression might move from verbal warning to written warning to suspension to termination over several months. Modified approaches might include more steps with shorter timeframes, immediate documentation requirements, or accelerated progression for safety-related violations.

Documentation requirements become even more critical with personality-disordered employees because their reactions to discipline may include legal challenges, grievance procedures, or attempts to manipulate the process. Every interaction should be documented with specific behavioral descriptions, witness information, and clear connections to established expectations.

Witness inclusion provides protection for both managers and employees during disciplinary discussions. Personality-disordered individuals may later claim conversations didn't occur, misrepresent what was said, or accuse managers of inappropriate behavior. Having neutral witnesses protects all parties while ensuring accurate records of disciplinary processes.

Safety considerations may require accelerated discipline timelines when personality disorder behaviors create risks for colleagues or clients. Traditional progressive discipline assumes time for improvement, but some personality disorder patterns pose immediate risks that can't wait for gradual behavior change.

Sarah, an HR manager, implemented modified progressive discipline with Robert, whose paranoid traits had created ongoing conflicts with colleagues and clients. Instead of standard verbal and written warnings separated by 30-60 days, she provided written documentation for every disciplinary conversation, included a neutral witness from senior management, and established 30-day review periods with specific behavioral targets. When Robert's suspicions about colleagues led to inappropriate investigation of their personal lives, Sarah moved immediately to final written warning due to privacy violations and harassment concerns.

Accommodation considerations require integrating reasonable accommodations into discipline procedures without excusing violations of essential job requirements. This might include modified timelines for individuals who need extra processing time, alternative communication methods for those with social anxieties, or structured support for boundary-setting challenges.

Appeal processes must account for personality disorder patterns that may include manipulation, victimization claims, or attempts to shift blame to others. Appeal procedures should include objective reviewers who understand personality disorder dynamics while maintaining fair hearing standards for all employees.

Training requirements for managers implementing progressive discipline with personality-disordered employees should cover legal compliance, documentation standards, safety assessment, and de-escalation techniques. Managers need specialized skills to navigate these complex situations effectively while protecting all parties' rights and interests.

Resource coordination involves connecting discipline processes with available support resources including employee assistance programs, mental health benefits, accommodation services, and legal consultation. This coordination ensures employees receive appropriate support while maintaining accountability for workplace performance and behavior.

7.3 Accommodation Integration in Performance Plans

Integrating reasonable accommodations into performance management requires balancing legal requirements with operational needs while maintaining fairness for all employees. This integration proves particularly challenging with personality disorders because accommodations must address symptoms without excusing behaviors that affect workplace safety or productivity.

Medical documentation provides the foundation for accommodation decisions, but personality disorder documentation may be less specific than accommodations for physical disabilities. Mental health professionals may recommend general accommodations like "reduced stress" or "flexible scheduling" without providing specific guidance about implementation or limitations.

Interactive process requirements mandate good-faith discussions between employers and employees about potential accommodations. This process must be individualized, considering the specific job requirements, workplace environment, and employee's particular symptoms and needs. Documentation of this process protects both parties and demonstrates compliance with legal requirements.

Essential function analysis determines which job requirements are fundamental and cannot be waived through accommodation. For personality-disordered employees, this analysis often focuses on interpersonal skills, teamwork requirements, communication standards, and safety-related behaviors that may be affected by their conditions.

Michael, a department supervisor, worked with Lisa, whose borderline personality disorder affected her emotional regulation and interpersonal relationships. The interactive process identified accommodations including private workspace to reduce social stimulation, structured feedback sessions with written summaries, flexible break schedules for emotional regulation, and modified conflict resolution procedures. However, essential functions remained unchanged: maintaining professional relationships with clients, meeting project deadlines, and following safety protocols. The accommodations helped Lisa manage her symptoms while preserving accountability for core job performance.

Limitation boundaries specify what accommodations cannot include while maintaining legal compliance and operational effectiveness.

These boundaries typically focus on fundamental job alterations, safety compromises, undue financial burdens, or accommodations that would negatively affect other employees' rights or working conditions.

Effectiveness monitoring tracks whether accommodations are achieving their intended purpose of enabling successful job performance. Regular review allows modification of accommodations that aren't working while identifying additional support needs that may emerge over time.

Colleague education may be necessary to help team members understand accommodation implementations without violating privacy requirements. This education focuses on behavioral expectations and team functioning rather than specific medical conditions or accommodation details.

Performance standards maintenance ensures that accommodated employees meet the same productivity and quality standards as their colleagues, even if they achieve these standards through different methods or with additional support. Accommodations change how work gets done, not the results expected.

7.4 When Traditional Approaches Don't Work

Some personality disorder situations prove resistant to conventional performance management and discipline approaches. These cases require specialized interventions that may include professional evaluation, alternative assignments, or consideration of employment termination when other options have been exhausted.

Escalation triggers signal when traditional approaches aren't working and additional interventions are needed. These might include repeated boundary violations despite clear expectations, safety incidents that could harm colleagues or clients, manipulation of support systems for personal advantage, or complete resistance to feedback and coaching efforts.

Professional evaluation may be necessary when personality disorder symptoms significantly impair job performance despite accommodation efforts. Fitness-for-duty evaluations can provide objective assessment of an employee's ability to perform essential job functions safely and effectively.

Alternative assignment considerations explore different roles or environments that might better match the individual's capabilities while addressing their limitations. This might include less interpersonally demanding positions, more structured environments, or roles with reduced decision-making responsibilities.

Team protection measures become necessary when personality-disordered individuals create ongoing disruption despite intervention efforts. These measures might include modified team compositions, structured interaction protocols, or limitation of the individual's participation in certain activities.

David, a project manager whose antisocial traits had created ongoing ethical violations and team conflicts, required escalated interventions when traditional discipline proved ineffective. Despite clear expectations, written warnings, and accommodation attempts, he continued manipulating project data, undermining colleagues, and violating client confidentiality. The organization arranged for fitness-for-duty evaluation, explored alternative assignments in roles with less interpersonal interaction, and ultimately concluded that his pattern of rule violations posed unacceptable risks that couldn't be managed through accommodation or discipline alone.

Legal consultation becomes essential when traditional approaches fail and termination consideration begins. Employment attorneys can provide guidance about documentation requirements, accommodation obligations, and termination procedures that minimize legal risks while protecting the organization's interests.

Support system coordination may include employee assistance programs, mental health benefits, outplacement services, and other resources that help individuals transition successfully while maintaining their dignity and well-being during difficult employment situations.

7.5 Termination Considerations and Risk Management

Employment termination of personality-disordered individuals requires careful analysis of legal risks, safety concerns, and procedural requirements. These terminations often involve higher complexity than typical employment separations due to accommodation requirements, potential disability claims, and unpredictable reactions from individuals whose conditions affect their judgment and emotional regulation.

Documentation review must demonstrate clear policy violations, failed improvement efforts, and exhausted accommodation options. The documentation should tell a compelling story that outside reviewers (including judges, juries, or arbitrators) can understand and evaluate fairly. Gaps in documentation or inconsistent enforcement can create legal vulnerabilities.

Legal compliance verification ensures all ADA requirements have been met, including interactive process obligations, reasonable accommodation considerations, and direct threat assessments when applicable. Legal review before termination can prevent costly mistakes and provide additional protection against discrimination claims.

Safety assessment evaluates potential risks associated with termination, including threats to colleagues, workplace violence potential, or self-harm concerns. Personality-disordered individuals may react unpredictably to employment loss, and organizations must consider these risks in termination planning and execution.

Termination procedures should be carefully planned to maximize safety while maintaining dignity for all involved. This might include timing considerations, security arrangements, witness presence, and communication scripts that avoid escalating emotional reactions while clearly conveying the termination decision.

Jennifer, an HR director, managed the termination of Marcus, whose narcissistic traits had created ongoing harassment complaints and client relationship problems. Despite extensive documentation, accommodation efforts, and progressive discipline, Marcus continued exploiting colleagues and violating professional boundaries. The termination procedure included legal review of all documentation, security consultation about potential risks, carefully scripted termination conversation with witness present, immediate removal of system access, and follow-up monitoring for several weeks to ensure no workplace contact or harassment of former colleagues.

Post-termination considerations may include reference policies, unemployment compensation responses, legal claim monitoring, and ongoing safety assessment. Some personality-disordered individuals may engage in prolonged disputes, harassment of former colleagues, or attempts to damage the organization's reputation through false claims or negative publicity.

Support for remaining employees helps teams recover from the disruption caused by problematic colleagues and the stress of termination processes. This support might include team debriefing sessions, individual counseling resources, modified workload distribution, and reassurance about organizational commitment to maintaining healthy workplace environments.

Learning integration involves analyzing what worked and what didn't work in the performance management process to improve future responses to similar situations. This analysis can inform policy development, training programs, and prevention strategies that reduce the likelihood of similar problems occurring.

Boundaries With Compassion

Performance management with personality-disordered employees requires walking a careful line between accountability and compassion, between legal compliance and human understanding. These individuals often struggle with conditions they didn't choose and may not fully understand, yet their behaviors can create real harm for colleagues and organizations.

The frameworks presented here acknowledge this complexity by providing structured approaches that maintain necessary boundaries while preserving human dignity. They recognize that some situations require firm action while others benefit from flexibility and accommodation. Most importantly, they provide clear procedures that protect everyone involved—the individual with personality disorders, their colleagues, and the organization.

Effective performance management in these situations requires patience, skill, and sometimes difficult decisions about employment continuation. However, organizations that develop these capabilities often find their overall management effectiveness improves as leaders become more skilled at setting clear expectations, providing appropriate support, and maintaining accountability for all employees.

The goal isn't to cure personality disorders through performance management but to create conditions where individuals can succeed within their capabilities while protecting the workplace environment for everyone. This balance serves both individual and organizational interests while maintaining the compassionate yet professional approach that complex human situations require.

Performance Management Essentials:

- Clear expectations and boundaries must be more specific for personality-disordered employees than for typical workers due to their difficulty interpreting social cues and workplace norms
- Progressive discipline requires modifications to account for rigid thinking patterns and defensive reactions that characterize personality disorders
- Accommodation integration must balance legal requirements with operational needs while maintaining fairness for all employees

- Alternative interventions become necessary when traditional approaches prove ineffective despite consistent implementation
- Termination decisions require careful legal review and safety assessment due to the complex reactions personality disorders can create
- Success requires balancing accountability with compassion while protecting all stakeholders' interests and rights

Chapter 8: Building Support Systems and Team Resilience

The oak tree that stands alone in the storm often falls, while the grove of trees with interconnected root systems weathers the same winds by supporting each other. Teams facing personality disorder challenges require similar interconnected support systems that distribute stress, share knowledge, and provide mutual protection during difficult periods. Building these support networks isn't about enabling dysfunction but creating resilient environments where everyone can thrive despite interpersonal challenges.

Effective support systems serve multiple functions: they prevent isolation of team members dealing with difficult colleagues, provide skill development for managing complex interpersonal situations, create early warning systems for emerging problems, and establish recovery mechanisms for teams that have experienced significant disruption. These systems must be intentionally designed and actively maintained to remain effective over time.

8.1 Team Composition and Role Design

Strategic team composition and thoughtful role design can significantly reduce personality disorder impacts while maximizing team effectiveness. Understanding how different personality types interact allows leaders to create team structures that minimize conflicts while leveraging individual strengths appropriately.

Personality disorder distribution affects team dynamics dramatically. Teams with multiple personality-disordered individuals often experience amplified dysfunction as different disorders trigger each other's symptoms. A narcissistic individual's grandiosity may trigger a borderline person's abandonment fears, while antisocial manipulation can intensify paranoid suspicions. Limiting personality disorder concentration prevents these negative feedback loops.

Complementary skill sets can offset some personality disorder limitations while maintaining team productivity. Pairing detail-oriented obsessive-compulsive individuals with big-picture thinkers can leverage perfectionist strengths while preventing analysis paralysis. Combining confident narcissistic personalities with more cautious team members can balance risk-taking with prudent decision-making.

Role boundary clarity becomes especially important when teams include personality-disordered individuals who may struggle with appropriate limits or exploit unclear expectations. Well-defined roles prevent overlap conflicts, reduce manipulation opportunities, and provide structure that supports better functioning from individuals who need external organization.

Communication structure design can minimize personality disorder triggers while maintaining information flow. This might include formal meeting protocols that prevent domination by attention-seeking individuals, structured feedback systems that reduce criticism sensitivity, or documented decision-making processes that address paranoid concerns about hidden agendas.

The engineering team at a software development company successfully integrated Robert, whose obsessive-compulsive personality traits had previously created bottlenecks and team conflicts. Team leader Sarah redesigned roles to leverage Robert's attention to detail in quality assurance while removing him from time-sensitive decision-making positions. She paired him with Maria, whose flexible thinking complemented his perfectionist standards. The team established clear protocols for code review that channeled Robert's thorough approach productively while preventing delays in release schedules. Weekly meetings included structured agenda items that satisfied Robert's need for detailed planning while maintaining focus on deliverable outcomes.

Supervision models may require modification when teams include personality-disordered individuals. Some may need closer oversight to prevent problematic behaviors, while others function better with minimal supervision that reduces feelings of being controlled or criticized. Understanding individual needs allows supervisors to provide appropriate support without creating additional stress.

Conflict resolution structures built into team design can address personality disorder-related disputes more effectively than ad hoc responses. These might include neutral mediators for interpersonal conflicts, structured problem-solving processes that prevent emotional escalation, or clear escalation procedures for situations that exceed team-level resolution capabilities.

Performance measurement systems must account for personality disorder impacts on traditional metrics while maintaining accountability standards. This might include team-based measures that distribute individual risk, outcome-focused metrics that allow flexibility in work methods, or behavioral indicators that track interpersonal functioning alongside productivity measures.

8.2 Creating Psychological Safety Despite Challenges

Psychological safety—the belief that team members can express ideas, ask questions, and admit mistakes without fear of negative consequences—becomes both more difficult and more important when teams include personality-disordered individuals. These individuals may create unpredictable reactions, interpersonal drama, or communication difficulties that undermine other team members' sense of safety and trust.

Foundation elements of psychological safety include predictable leadership responses, fair treatment standards, open communication norms, and support for learning from mistakes. Each element requires special attention when personality disorders are present because these conditions can disrupt normal trust-building processes.

Leadership modeling proves especially crucial because team members watch how leaders respond to personality disorder challenges. Leaders who remain calm during emotional outbursts, maintain consistent standards despite manipulation attempts, and provide fair treatment regardless of personal relationships demonstrate the stability that psychological safety requires.

Communication norms must be explicitly established and consistently enforced to prevent personality disorder behaviors from dominating team interactions. This might include meeting facilitation rules that ensure everyone gets heard, conflict resolution protocols that prevent personal attacks, or feedback systems that maintain professional boundaries.

Trust building activities require modification when personality disorders are present. Traditional team-building exercises that encourage vulnerability may trigger defensive reactions or provide manipulation opportunities. More effective approaches focus on professional competence demonstration, collaborative problem-solving, and structured interaction opportunities that build confidence gradually.

Michael, a department manager in a financial services firm, created psychological safety in a team that included Jennifer, whose borderline traits had previously created emotional volatility and interpersonal drama. He established clear communication norms including "one person speaks at a time," "focus on work issues rather than personal reactions," and "schedule individual meetings for concerns that feel personal." He modeled calm responses to Jennifer's occasional emotional outbursts while maintaining consistent expectations for professional behavior. He created structured opportunities for team members to showcase their expertise and collaborate on projects without forced personal disclosure. Over six months, team trust improved significantly as members learned they could rely on consistent leadership and fair treatment despite ongoing interpersonal challenges.

Inclusion strategies ensure that all team members feel valued and heard despite personality disorder impacts on group dynamics. This requires active facilitation to prevent domination by attention-seeking individuals while drawing out contributions from more reserved team members who might withdraw in response to interpersonal tension.

Mistake handling protocols become crucial when personality disorders affect how individuals respond to errors or criticism. Some personality types may react with shame, rage, or blame-shifting that disrupts learning opportunities. Clear protocols for addressing mistakes focus on problem-solving rather than fault-finding while maintaining accountability standards.

Support resource awareness helps team members know where to turn when personality disorder impacts affect their well-being or performance. This includes both formal resources (HR, employee assistance programs, mental health benefits) and informal support networks (peer mentoring, professional development, team backup systems).

8.3 Peer Support and Mentoring Programs

Peer support and mentoring programs provide crucial assistance for teams managing personality disorder challenges while promoting professional development and resilience building. These programs must be carefully structured to provide genuine support without becoming gossip networks or complaint circles that reinforce negative dynamics.

Peer support structure focuses on professional skill development and stress management rather than personality analysis or complaint sharing. Effective programs teach colleagues how to maintain professional relationships, set appropriate boundaries, manage their own stress responses, and seek appropriate resources when situations exceed their capabilities.

Mentor training must include education about personality disorders, communication strategies, boundary setting, and resource identification. Mentors need skills for supporting colleagues without becoming amateur therapists or enforcement agents. They must understand their role limitations and know when to refer situations to professional resources.

Confidentiality protocols protect both individuals receiving support and those being discussed while maintaining necessary information sharing for safety and effectiveness. These protocols must balance privacy protection with practical collaboration needs while avoiding secrets that could undermine team trust.

Skill development focus ensures peer support programs build capabilities rather than just providing emotional venting opportunities. This might include communication skills training, stress management techniques, assertiveness development, or professional networking that builds career resilience beyond current team situations.

The marketing department at a consumer goods company developed a peer mentoring program after several team members expressed stress about working with Patricia, whose histrionic traits created ongoing interpersonal drama. The program paired experienced employees with newer team members to provide guidance about professional development, communication strategies, and resource utilization. Mentors received training about maintaining professional boundaries, supporting colleagues without enabling dysfunction, and recognizing when situations required management intervention. The program included monthly group sessions focused on skill development topics like "Managing Difficult Conversations," "Setting Professional Boundaries," and "Building Career Resilience." Participation was voluntary, and discussions focused on professional growth rather than individual complaints. Over time, team members developed stronger skills for managing challenging interpersonal situations while building supportive professional relationships.

Resource coordination connects peer support programs with formal organizational resources including HR guidance, employee assistance programs, training opportunities, and career development systems. This coordination ensures peer support complements rather than replaces professional resources while providing multiple avenues for assistance.

Outcome measurement tracks program effectiveness through metrics like participant satisfaction, skill development assessment, stress level monitoring, and team functioning indicators. Regular evaluation allows program modification and improvement while demonstrating value to organizational leadership.

Sustainability planning ensures peer support programs continue functioning despite personnel changes, budget constraints, or organizational restructuring. This includes training multiple mentors, developing program documentation, securing leadership support, and building programs into organizational culture rather than treating them as temporary initiatives.

8.4 Managing Team Dynamics Around Difficult Members

Team dynamics inevitably shift when personality-disordered individuals join groups, requiring proactive management to prevent dysfunction from spreading while maintaining productivity and morale. Understanding these dynamic changes allows leaders to intervene early and implement protective strategies.

Alliance formation patterns often emerge as team members develop different relationships with personality-disordered colleagues. Some may align with the difficult individual to avoid becoming targets, others may form protective coalitions against them, and some attempt to maintain neutrality. These alliances can create subdivisions that undermine team cohesion and effectiveness.

Communication adaptation occurs as teams modify their interaction patterns to accommodate personality disorder impacts. This might include elaborate information sharing systems to prevent manipulation, careful language choices to avoid triggering emotional reactions, or informal warning systems about mood states and behavioral patterns. While these adaptations may be necessary for functioning, they also represent energy diverted from productive work activities.

Productivity compensation happens when capable team members work harder to offset personality disorder impacts on overall performance. This compensation may mask problems temporarily but creates burnout risk and resentment that eventually surfaces in turnover or performance decline among the most productive employees.

Meeting dynamics require special management when personality disorders affect group interactions. This might include structured agendas that prevent domination, facilitation techniques that ensure participation from all members, or ground rules that maintain professional focus despite interpersonal tensions.

David, a project team leader in a consulting firm, managed complex dynamics created by Marcus, whose narcissistic traits had gradually divided the team into competing factions. Some members aligned with Marcus to gain access to his technical expertise and avoid his criticism, while others resented his self-promotion and credit-taking behaviors. David implemented structured meeting protocols including rotating leadership roles, mandatory agenda items for each team member, and documented decision-making processes that prevented post-meeting disputes. He established individual check-ins with each team member to monitor stress levels and provide support without creating gossip opportunities. He redirected competitive energy toward external goals (client satisfaction, project innovation) rather than internal status struggles. Over several months, team cohesion improved as members focused on shared professional objectives rather than interpersonal positioning.

Conflict prevention strategies address personality disorder triggers before they create team-wide problems. This might include environmental modifications that reduce stress, communication protocols that minimize misunderstandings, or workload distribution that accounts for individual capabilities and limitations.

Intervention timing becomes crucial because personality disorder impacts often escalate gradually until crisis points are reached. Early intervention during minor incidents proves more effective than crisis management after major disruptions have occurred. Team leaders must develop sensitivity to escalation patterns and intervene proactively.

Recovery planning prepares teams for managing aftermath when personality disorder incidents do occur despite prevention efforts. This includes damage control procedures, relationship repair strategies, and morale restoration activities that help teams move forward constructively rather than remaining stuck in negative dynamics.

8.5 Recovery Strategies After Toxic Employee Departure

Teams that have experienced significant personality disorder impacts often require intentional recovery strategies to rebuild trust, restore productivity, and prevent lasting damage to team culture. Recovery isn't automatic—it requires active leadership and systematic approaches to address the various ways that toxic behaviors can continue affecting teams even after problematic individuals leave.

Damage assessment identifies specific areas where personality disorder impacts have affected team functioning. This might include relationship conflicts that outlasted the individual's presence, modified work processes that are no longer necessary, communication patterns that became defensive or formal, or productivity systems that developed to compensate for dysfunction.

Relationship repair addresses interpersonal conflicts and trust issues that developed during the difficult period. Team members may have taken sides, shared confidential information, or developed negative opinions about colleagues' behavior during stressful situations. Repair processes focus on professional relationship restoration rather than personal friendship building.

Culture restoration rebuilds positive team norms and values that may have eroded during periods of significant dysfunction. This includes reestablishing communication openness, collaborative problem-solving, mutual support, and shared commitment to team success rather than individual protection.

Process modification removes or adjusts systems that were created to manage personality disorder impacts but are no longer needed for effective team functioning. This might include excessive documentation requirements, formal communication protocols, or oversight procedures that were necessary during crisis periods but now inhibit normal productivity.

The customer service team at a telecommunications company required extensive recovery support after Patricia's departure. Her histrionic traits had created eighteen months of interpersonal drama that divided the team, reduced productivity, and damaged client relationships. Team leader Sarah implemented a systematic recovery process beginning with individual conversations to assess each member's experience and concerns. She facilitated team meetings focused on rebuilding professional relationships and establishing new communication norms. She eliminated documentation requirements and oversight procedures that had been implemented to manage Patricia's behavior. She arranged team training on effective communication and conflict resolution to rebuild collaborative skills. Most importantly, she consistently reinforced positive interactions and team achievements to restore confidence in the team's ability to function effectively together.

Skill rebuilding helps team members recover interpersonal and professional capabilities that may have been suppressed during periods of significant dysfunction. Individuals may have become conflict-avoidant, stopped sharing ideas, or developed defensive communication patterns that need conscious modification to restore full effectiveness.

Trust restoration requires time and consistent demonstration that the team environment has genuinely improved. Leaders must model trustworthy behavior, maintain consistent standards, and provide positive reinforcement for collaborative behaviors while addressing any remaining negative patterns quickly and effectively.

Prevention implementation ensures teams develop resilience against future personality disorder challenges. This includes early warning system development, improved hiring and onboarding processes, enhanced training for managing difficult situations, and stronger organizational support systems that prevent problems from escalating to crisis levels.

Success celebration acknowledges the team's resilience and recovery achievements while building confidence for future challenges. Recognition of progress motivates continued positive behavior and demonstrates organizational value for healthy team functioning. Celebration also helps shift focus from past problems to future possibilities and achievements.

The Strength of Connection

Building support systems and team resilience around personality disorder challenges reveals fundamental truths about human workplace relationships. We are not isolated individuals who happen to work in the same building—we are interconnected beings whose well-being and effectiveness depend significantly on the quality of our professional relationships and support networks.

The strategies presented here recognize that personality disorders affect entire teams, not just the individuals who have these conditions. They acknowledge that recovery and resilience require intentional effort and systematic approaches rather than hoping that time alone will heal interpersonal wounds or restore team effectiveness.

Most importantly, these approaches build capabilities that serve teams well beyond personality disorder situations. The communication skills, boundary-setting abilities, conflict resolution techniques, and mutual support systems that help teams manage difficult colleagues also improve overall team performance, job satisfaction, and organizational resilience.

Organizations that invest in building these support systems often discover that their workplace cultures become more robust, their employees more skilled at managing interpersonal challenges, and their teams more capable of weathering various types of difficulties. The investment pays dividends far beyond the immediate situations that prompted their development.

The goal isn't to create perfect teams without interpersonal challenges but to build resilient teams that can maintain effectiveness and well-being despite the inevitable human complexities that arise in any workplace. This resilience serves everyone's interests while creating environments where individuals can thrive regardless of the personality challenges they may face.

Support System Foundations:

- Strategic team composition and role design can minimize personality disorder impacts while maximizing individual strengths and team effectiveness
- Psychological safety requires special attention and active maintenance when personality disorders create unpredictable interpersonal dynamics
- Peer support and mentoring programs provide crucial assistance while building professional skills and career resilience
- Team dynamics require proactive management to prevent personality disorder impacts from spreading throughout groups
- Recovery strategies after toxic employee departure must be systematic and sustained to rebuild trust and restore healthy team functioning
- Effective support systems serve teams well beyond personality disorder situations by building general resilience and interpersonal capabilities

Chapter 9: Personal Boundaries and Self-Protection

The skilled surgeon doesn't operate without gloves, masks, and protective equipment—not because they fear their patients, but because they understand that protection allows them to provide better care while maintaining their own health and effectiveness. Similarly, working with personality-disordered colleagues requires protective strategies that safeguard your well-being while enabling you to remain professional, productive, and engaged in your work.

Self-protection isn't about building walls or becoming defensive—it's about developing the skills and strategies that allow you to thrive in challenging interpersonal environments. These techniques protect your mental health, preserve your career trajectory, and maintain your ability to contribute meaningfully to your organization while working alongside individuals whose conditions create ongoing workplace difficulties.

9.1 The Art of Professional Boundaries

Professional boundaries represent invisible lines that define appropriate workplace relationships, communication patterns, and behavioral expectations. With personality-disordered colleagues, these boundaries require more intentional establishment and consistent maintenance because these individuals often struggle to recognize or respect normal interpersonal limits.

Boundary types include emotional boundaries that protect your mental well-being, time boundaries that preserve your productivity, information boundaries that control what you share and receive, and physical boundaries that maintain appropriate workspace relationships. Each type requires different strategies and enforcement approaches.

Emotional boundaries protect you from absorbing others' intense emotions, manipulation attempts, or psychological drama. This means recognizing that their emotional storms don't require your participation, their crises don't automatically become your emergencies, and their interpretations of events don't need to shape your reality.

Time boundaries preserve your ability to complete your work without being constantly interrupted by colleagues who demand excessive attention, create unnecessary drama, or generate work problems through their dysfunction. This includes limiting time spent managing others' emotional needs, restricting availability for non-work conversations, and protecting scheduled work time from interpersonal interruptions.

Information boundaries control what personal or professional information you share while limiting how much of others' information you're willing to receive. This means avoiding oversharing about your personal life, declining invitations to hear gossip or complaints about colleagues, and maintaining professional topic focus during workplace interactions.

Physical boundaries maintain appropriate workspace relationships including personal space, physical contact, and environmental comfort. Some personality-disordered individuals may invade personal space, touch inappropriately, or create uncomfortable physical dynamics that require clear, consistent limit-setting.

Sarah, a marketing coordinator, successfully established boundaries with Jennifer, whose borderline traits had previously created emotional chaos and productivity disruptions. Sarah stopped engaging with Jennifer's emotional crises during work hours, instead saying "I can see you're upset, and I hope you find the support you need. Right now I need to focus on the campaign deadline." She limited personal conversations to brief exchanges, redirected excessive emotional sharing with "That sounds difficult—have you considered talking to someone in HR or the employee assistance program?" She maintained consistent responses regardless of Jennifer's emotional state, avoiding the roller coaster of being idealized one day and devalued the next. Most importantly, Sarah stopped trying to "fix" Jennifer's problems or provide therapy-like support that was beyond her role and capabilities.

Boundary establishment requires clear, direct communication about your limits without extensive justification or apology. Effective boundary statements include "I'm not able to discuss personal matters during work time," "I need to focus on my projects during lunch break," or "I prefer to keep our conversations focused on work topics."

Boundary maintenance proves more challenging than initial establishment because personality-disordered individuals often test limits repeatedly, escalate when boundaries are enforced, or use emotional manipulation to weaken your resolve. Consistent enforcement requires treating boundary violations as information about their behavior rather than invitations to negotiate or explain your limits repeatedly.

Common boundary challenges include guilt when enforcing limits with individuals who seem needy or distressed, pressure from colleagues who think you're being "mean" or "unsupportive," and exhaustion from constantly having to reinforce the same boundaries repeatedly. Understanding these challenges helps you prepare responses and maintain consistency despite social pressure.

Boundary flexibility allows appropriate adjustments based on circumstances while maintaining core protective limits. This might mean providing extra support during genuine crises while refusing to enable ongoing drama, or offering professional assistance while declining to serve as an unpaid therapist for personality disorder symptoms.

9.2 Recognizing and Responding to Manipulation

Manipulation involves attempts to control others' behavior, emotions, or decisions through deception, emotional pressure, or exploitation of relationships. Personality-disordered individuals often use manipulation as their primary interpersonal strategy, making recognition and response skills essential for self-protection.

Manipulation tactics vary by personality disorder type but often include guilt-tripping, gaslighting, triangulation, emotional blackmail, playing victim, and exploiting others' empathy or sense of obligation. Understanding these tactics helps you recognize when they're being used against you rather than accepting them as normal communication patterns.

Guilt manipulation involves making you feel responsible for others' emotional states, work problems, or life difficulties. Statements like "You're the only one who understands me," "I can't handle this project without your help," or "You're being selfish by not helping me" are designed to override your boundaries through emotional pressure.

Gaslighting makes you question your own perceptions, memories, or judgments through persistent denial, contradiction, or reframing of events. This might include claiming conversations never happened, insisting you misunderstood clearly stated information, or suggesting your emotional reactions are unreasonable or oversensitive.

Triangulation involves bringing third parties into conflicts to create pressure, confusion, or divided loyalties. This includes sharing confidential information to gain allies, creating competitions between colleagues, or using authority figures to pressure you into compliance with their demands.

Playing victim portrays the manipulator as helpless, wronged, or unfairly treated to gain sympathy and support while avoiding accountability for their behavior. This tactic often includes exaggerating difficulties, minimizing their own contributions to problems, or claiming persecution when facing normal consequences.

Michael, an IT specialist, learned to recognize and respond to manipulation from David, whose antisocial traits included sophisticated exploitation of colleagues' goodwill and professional obligations. David would approach Michael with urgent "emergencies" that required immediate attention, claiming that system failures would cost the company thousands of dollars if not addressed instantly. When Michael investigated, these emergencies often proved to be routine maintenance or non-critical issues that David had created through poor planning. David would then guilt-trip Michael about "not being a team player" when he questioned the urgency. Michael learned to respond by verifying information independently, asking for written documentation of emergency requests, and insisting on following standard prioritization procedures regardless of David's emotional pressure tactics.

Response strategies for manipulation include recognizing the tactic being used, refusing to accept guilt or responsibility for others' problems, maintaining focus on facts rather than emotions, and declining to participate in triangulation or drama creation. Effective responses often involve asking clarifying questions, requesting written documentation, or suggesting appropriate resources rather than providing immediate compliance.

Information verification becomes essential when working with manipulative individuals because they often distort facts, misrepresent situations, or fabricate urgency to gain compliance. This means checking information independently, confirming details with other sources, and avoiding decision-making based solely on manipulative individuals' representations.

Emotional regulation helps you maintain clear thinking when facing manipulation attempts. This includes recognizing your emotional reactions as information rather than imperatives for action, taking time to process requests before responding, and seeking consultation when feeling pressured to make immediate decisions.

Documentation practices protect you from later manipulation attempts that may include claims about agreements that were never made, promises that were never offered, or conversations that never occurred. Keeping records of interactions, following up verbal agreements with written confirmation, and copying appropriate parties on important communications all provide protection against manipulation.

9.3 Documentation as Self-Protection

Strategic documentation serves as your professional insurance policy when working with personality-disordered individuals who may later misrepresent events, file false complaints, or create legal challenges for colleagues who refuse to enable their dysfunction. Effective documentation tells your professional story accurately while protecting against manipulation and false accusations.

Documentation purposes include protecting against false accusations, providing evidence of professional conduct, tracking patterns of problematic behavior, supporting accommodation discussions, and creating records for potential legal proceedings. Understanding these purposes helps you focus documentation efforts on information that serves protective functions.

Documentation standards require objective language, specific behavioral descriptions, dates and circumstances, witness information when available, and focus on work-related impacts rather than personal characteristics or psychological interpretations. Good documentation reads like professional journalism rather than personal opinion or emotional reaction.

Timing considerations affect documentation quality and legal protection. Immediate documentation captures details accurately but may not be practical during workplace interactions. Daily summaries provide balance between accuracy and practicality while weekly reviews help identify patterns that individual incidents might not reveal.

Format options include email summaries sent to yourself, formal incident reports, detailed calendar entries, or structured documentation logs. The format should match your organization's culture while providing adequate detail for potential future reference.

Email summaries often work well because they create timestamped records that are difficult to dispute later.

Content guidelines focus on observable behaviors rather than interpretations, specific quotes rather than general characterizations, and factual impacts rather than emotional reactions. Effective documentation includes what was said or done, when and where it occurred, who was present, and what professional impacts resulted from the interaction.

Lisa, a project manager, developed comprehensive documentation practices after experiencing manipulation and false accusations from Robert, whose paranoid traits led to distorted interpretations of normal workplace interactions. She began sending email summaries after meetings that included "As we discussed in today's project meeting, the agreed timeline for deliverables is [specific dates], the assigned responsibilities are [specific tasks for each team member], and the next check-in is scheduled for [specific date and time]." She documented concerning behaviors objectively: "During the team meeting on [date], Robert stated that he believes colleagues are monitoring his computer usage to find reasons for termination. When I explained that the new software installation requires temporary monitoring for technical troubleshooting, he responded that he 'doesn't trust anyone in this company.' This conversation occurred in front of [witnesses] and delayed project discussion for 15 minutes." This documentation later proved essential when Robert filed complaints claiming Lisa had harassed him and violated his privacy.

Legal protection requires documentation that could support your position in potential grievance procedures, discrimination claims, or legal proceedings. This means maintaining professional language, avoiding emotional reactions or personal opinions, and focusing on job-related impacts rather than personality characteristics.

Privacy considerations affect what information you can document and how you can share it with others. Personal medical information about colleagues should never be included in your documentation, and sharing should be limited to individuals with legitimate business needs for the information.

Storage and security protect your documentation from unauthorized access while ensuring availability when needed. This might include password-protected files, encrypted storage systems, or secure physical filing systems depending on your organization's policies and your personal preferences.

Professional consultation helps you determine what should be documented, how to maintain objectivity, and when documentation might support formal complaints or legal action. HR professionals, employee assistance counselors, or legal advisors can provide guidance about documentation practices that protect your interests while maintaining compliance with organizational policies.

9.4 Building Your Support Network

Working with personality-disordered individuals can create isolation, self-doubt, and emotional exhaustion that affect both your professional performance and personal well-being. Building a robust support network provides perspective, practical assistance, and emotional support that help you maintain effectiveness while protecting your mental health.

Support network components include professional mentors, trusted colleagues, HR resources, external advisors, personal friends and family, and mental health professionals. Each component serves different functions and provides different types of assistance depending on your specific needs and circumstances.

Professional mentors offer career guidance, workplace navigation advice, and objective perspective on challenging situations. Mentors can help you assess whether your experiences are normal workplace challenges or signs of dysfunction requiring intervention. They also provide guidance about career decisions, skill development, and professional relationship management.

Trusted colleagues provide day-to-day support, reality-checking, and collaborative problem-solving. These relationships offer validation that your perceptions are accurate, assistance with work challenges, and social connection that counteracts isolation created by difficult interpersonal situations.

HR resources include employee assistance programs, accommodation services, grievance procedures, and policy guidance. These resources provide formal support systems and professional expertise for addressing workplace challenges while protecting your rights and interests.

External advisors might include employment attorneys, career coaches, professional counselors, or industry mentors who can provide objective perspective and specialized expertise. External advisors offer viewpoints unconstrained by organizational politics or relationships.

Personal relationships with friends and family provide emotional support, stress relief, and perspective that extends beyond workplace concerns. These relationships help maintain psychological balance and prevent work challenges from overwhelming your entire life experience.

Jennifer, a software developer, built a comprehensive support network after experiencing ongoing manipulation and emotional volatility from Patricia, whose histrionic traits had created a toxic team environment. Jennifer cultivated mentoring relationships with senior developers in other departments who provided career guidance and objective perspective on her situation. She developed trusting relationships with two colleagues who could verify her perceptions and provide mutual support during difficult interactions with Patricia. She accessed the employee assistance program for counseling support and contacted HR for guidance about documentation and accommodation options. She consulted with an employment attorney to understand her rights and options if the situation escalated. Most importantly, she maintained strong personal relationships that provided emotional support and helped her maintain perspective about the temporary nature of workplace challenges compared to her overall life and career trajectory.

Network activation requires knowing when and how to access different support resources based on your specific needs and circumstances. This includes understanding confidentiality limitations, appropriate timing for different types of consultation, and how to frame requests for assistance in ways that maximize helpfulness.

Reciprocity maintenance ensures your support relationships remain balanced and sustainable over time. This means providing support to others when appropriate, expressing gratitude for assistance received, and avoiding over-reliance on any single support source that could create burden or dependency.

Confidentiality management protects sensitive information while allowing appropriate sharing for support purposes. This includes understanding what information can be shared with different support sources, how to discuss workplace challenges without violating organizational policies, and when professional confidentiality requirements might limit support options.

Resource evaluation helps you assess which support sources are most helpful for different types of challenges while identifying gaps that might need additional resources. Regular evaluation ensures your support network remains current and effective as circumstances change.

9.5 When to Consider Legal Consultation

Legal consultation becomes necessary when workplace situations involving personality-disordered individuals create potential legal risks, violate employment protections, or require formal intervention beyond standard HR procedures. Understanding when to seek legal advice protects your rights while helping you make informed decisions about workplace challenges.

Consultation triggers include harassment or discrimination based on protected characteristics, retaliation for reporting problematic behavior, safety threats or violent incidents, wrongful termination concerns, or violations of accommodation rights. These situations may require legal expertise to protect your interests and understand your options.

Harassment patterns that may warrant legal consultation include persistent unwelcome behavior based on protected characteristics, creation of hostile work environments, sexual harassment or inappropriate advances, or discriminatory treatment related to mental health conditions or accommodation requests.

Retaliation concerns arise when you face negative consequences for reporting personality disorder-related problems, requesting accommodations, filing complaints, or refusing to participate in inappropriate behaviors. Retaliation can include termination, demotion, schedule changes, assignment modifications, or social isolation orchestrated by management.

Safety issues require immediate legal consultation when personality-disordered individuals make threats, engage in stalking behaviors, commit acts of violence, or create conditions where you fear for your physical safety. These situations may require both legal action and law enforcement involvement.

Documentation preparation for legal consultation should include chronological incident records, email communications, witness information, policy violations, and impacts on your employment or well-being. Organized documentation helps attorneys assess your situation efficiently while providing evidence for potential legal action.

Mark, an accountant, sought legal consultation after experiencing escalating harassment from David, whose antisocial traits had evolved into increasingly concerning behavior patterns. David had begun making veiled threats about "making life difficult" for colleagues who questioned his work, following Mark to his car after work, and spreading false rumors about Mark's competence and professional conduct. When Mark reported these concerns to HR, David's behavior initially improved but then escalated to include explicit threats about "teaching lessons" to "troublemakers." Mark's attorney helped him document the pattern of escalating behavior, guided him through filing formal complaints with appropriate agencies, and provided representation during HR investigations. The legal consultation proved essential when David was terminated and subsequently filed false claims against Mark and other colleagues who had reported his behavior.

Consultation timing affects the quality of legal advice and your strategic options. Early consultation often provides more alternatives and preventive strategies, while delayed consultation may limit options to reactive damage control. Consulting before situations reach crisis levels typically produces better outcomes.

Attorney selection should focus on employment law specialists who understand workplace mental health issues, personality disorder dynamics, and relevant federal and state protections. Experience with similar cases and knowledge of local employment laws and court systems provide significant advantages.

Cost considerations include consultation fees, potential litigation expenses, and time investments required for legal proceedings. Many employment attorneys offer initial consultations at reduced rates and may work on contingency fees for certain types of cases. Understanding cost structures helps you make informed decisions about legal representation.

Alternative resolution options may include mediation, arbitration, or administrative complaints that provide faster, less expensive alternatives to litigation while still protecting your rights and interests. Legal consultation helps you understand which approaches might be most effective for your specific situation.

Prevention strategies discussed during legal consultation can help you avoid future problems while protecting your current position.

This might include documentation improvements, communication modifications, or strategic career moves that reduce legal risks while advancing your professional objectives.

Standing Your Ground

Self-protection in challenging workplace environments requires courage, skill, and strategic thinking that goes far beyond simply trying to "get along" with difficult colleagues. The strategies presented here acknowledge that you have the right to work in environments free from harassment, manipulation, and abuse—regardless of others' mental health conditions or personal challenges.

Implementing these protection strategies often feels uncomfortable initially because they require you to prioritize your own well-being over others' emotional needs or demands. This discomfort is normal and usually indicates that you've been trained to accommodate dysfunction rather than maintain healthy boundaries. Learning to trust your perceptions, enforce appropriate limits, and seek help when needed are skills that serve you throughout your career.

The goal isn't to become defensive, suspicious, or adversarial in your workplace relationships. Instead, these strategies help you maintain professionalism while protecting yourself from individuals whose conditions create ongoing interpersonal challenges. This protection allows you to remain compassionate and collaborative with colleagues who reciprocate appropriate workplace relationships.

Self-protection skills also prepare you for future workplace challenges that may not involve personality disorders but require similar boundary-setting, documentation, and support-seeking capabilities. Organizations and individuals change over time, and the skills you develop managing current challenges often prove helpful in unexpected future situations.

Most importantly, protecting yourself preserves your ability to contribute meaningfully to your work and organization. You can't serve others effectively if you're constantly managing your own survival in toxic interpersonal environments. Self-protection creates the stability and confidence necessary for professional growth and meaningful contribution.

Personal Protection Framework:

- Professional boundaries require intentional establishment and consistent maintenance to protect against personality disorder impacts on your well-being and productivity
- Manipulation recognition and response skills prevent exploitation while maintaining professional relationships with challenging colleagues
- Strategic documentation provides protection against false accusations and manipulation while supporting formal intervention when necessary
- Comprehensive support networks offer perspective, practical assistance, and emotional support essential for managing difficult workplace situations
- Legal consultation becomes necessary when situations escalate beyond normal workplace challenges or violate employment protections
- Self-protection skills serve broader career purposes beyond current personality disorder challenges

Chapter 10: Strategic Communication for Self-Preservation

The air traffic controller doesn't engage in casual conversation with pilots during emergency landings—communication becomes precise, minimal, and focused solely on essential information that ensures safety and successful outcomes. Similarly, working with personality-disordered colleagues often requires shifting from normal workplace communication to protective strategies that minimize conflict while preserving your professional effectiveness and personal well-being.

Strategic communication isn't about becoming cold or manipulative—it's about adapting your communication style to achieve productive outcomes while protecting yourself from the emotional volatility, manipulation, and interpersonal drama that personality disorders often create. These techniques help you maintain professionalism while reducing your exposure to psychological stress and workplace conflict.

10.1 The Gray Rock Method: When and How

The Gray Rock method involves becoming as uninteresting and unresponsive as possible during interactions with individuals who thrive on drama, attention, or emotional reactions. Like a gray rock that attracts no attention in a field of stones, you become a boring, unremarkable presence that doesn't provide the stimulation that personality-disordered individuals often seek from their interpersonal relationships.

Method principles include providing minimal responses, avoiding emotional reactions, sharing no personal information, maintaining neutral facial expressions, and declining to participate in drama or conflict. The goal is to become so unremarkable that the personality-disordered individual loses interest and directs their attention elsewhere.

Appropriate situations for Gray Rock include interactions with narcissistic individuals who seek admiration or attention, histrionic personalities who create drama for excitement, antisocial individuals who exploit emotional reactions, or any personality-disordered colleague who seems to gain energy from interpersonal conflict or emotional intensity.

Implementation techniques require practice and consistency to be effective. This includes using single-word responses when possible, avoiding follow-up questions that encourage continued interaction, maintaining neutral body language and facial expressions, and declining invitations to share opinions or personal information.

Verbal responses should be factual, brief, and emotionally neutral. Examples include "Okay," "I understand," "That's interesting," or "I need to focus on my work now." Avoid providing detailed explanations, emotional reactions, or personal opinions that might encourage continued interaction or argument.

Non-verbal communication should reinforce your disinterest in extended interaction. This includes limited eye contact, neutral facial expressions, closed body posture that suggests you're focused on other tasks, and minimal physical movement or gesturing that might attract attention.

Sandra, a marketing analyst, successfully used Gray Rock techniques with Jennifer, whose histrionic traits had previously drawn Sandra into hours of workplace drama and emotional conversations. When Jennifer approached with her latest relationship crisis or workplace complaint, Sandra responded with brief acknowledgments like "I see" or "That sounds difficult" without asking follow-up questions or offering advice. She maintained focus on her computer screen or work materials, providing minimal eye contact and neutral facial expressions. When Jennifer tried to escalate the conversation with more dramatic details, Sandra responded with "I need to finish this report" and returned to her work. Over several weeks, Jennifer began seeking attention from other colleagues who provided more engaging responses, leaving Sandra free to focus on her professional responsibilities.

Boundary integration combines Gray Rock techniques with clear professional boundaries to create comprehensive protection. This might include statements like "I need to focus on work during office hours" delivered in a neutral, factual tone that doesn't invite argument or emotional reaction.

Consistency requirements mean using Gray Rock techniques every time, not just when you feel like it or when the personality-disordered individual is being particularly difficult. Inconsistent application can actually increase attention-seeking behavior as the individual works harder to regain the emotional engagement they previously received.

Limitations and risks include potential misunderstanding by colleagues who don't understand your strategy, possible escalation if the personality-disordered individual becomes frustrated by your lack of response, and emotional toll of maintaining neutral responses when you might naturally want to help or engage with distressed colleagues.

Professional balance ensures Gray Rock techniques don't interfere with necessary work collaboration or professional relationships. You can be emotionally neutral without being professionally unresponsive to legitimate work requests or collaborative needs.

10.2 Email Strategies and Written Documentation

Email communication provides unique advantages when working with personality-disordered colleagues because it creates permanent records, allows careful word choice, reduces emotional reactivity, and provides time for thoughtful responses. However, email also creates opportunities for misinterpretation, manipulation, and evidence that could be used against you if not handled strategically.

Email advantages include time to compose thoughtful responses, permanent records of communications, reduced emotional intensity compared to face-to-face interactions, ability to copy appropriate parties for transparency, and protection against later claims about what was or wasn't communicated.

Strategic composition involves writing emails that serve multiple purposes: communicating necessary information, protecting against manipulation, documenting important interactions, and maintaining professional relationships. This requires balancing clarity with caution, completeness with conciseness.

Professional tone remains consistent regardless of the emotional content or manipulative attempts in incoming emails. Your responses should maintain neutral, factual language even when responding to emotional outbursts, accusations, or manipulation attempts. This consistency protects your professional reputation while avoiding escalation.

Information control involves sharing only necessary work-related information while avoiding personal details, opinions about colleagues, or emotional reactions that could be used against you later. Treat every email as potentially public information that could be shared with supervisors, HR, or legal representatives.

Response timing can be used strategically to avoid immediate emotional reactions while demonstrating professional responsiveness. Waiting several hours before responding to emotionally charged emails allows you to craft measured responses while avoiding the appearance of being unresponsive or unprofessional.

Michael, a project coordinator, developed effective email strategies for managing David, whose antisocial traits included manipulation and exploitation of workplace relationships. When David sent urgent emails demanding immediate responses to non-critical issues, Michael responded within 24 hours with factual information and clear timelines: "I received your request for the quarterly report data. The standard timeline for this information is five business days from the request date. I will have the data available by [specific date] and will send it to you then." When David tried to escalate through emotional pressure or claims about emergency deadlines, Michael copied his supervisor and responded factually: "As discussed in our team meeting on [date], all quarterly reports follow the established timeline unless specifically designated as emergency requests through the standard exception process." This approach prevented manipulation while maintaining professional responsiveness and creating clear documentation of reasonable communication patterns.

Copy strategies involve including appropriate parties on emails to ensure transparency and prevent later manipulation or misrepresentation. This might include supervisors for important decisions, HR for policy-related issues, or colleagues for collaborative projects. However, avoid over-copying that could appear gossipy or unprofessional.

Documentation value of emails depends on professional language, factual content, and clear connection to work-related issues. Emails that could serve as evidence in future proceedings should focus on observable behaviors, specific incidents, and professional impacts rather than personal opinions or emotional reactions.

Security considerations include understanding your organization's email policies, retention requirements, and potential monitoring that could affect privacy expectations. Some organizations have policies about personal use of company email systems or retention of email communications that could affect your documentation strategies.

Response protocols for different types of problematic emails help you maintain consistency while protecting your interests. This might include standard responses for manipulation attempts, escalation procedures for threatening communications, or professional consultation for emails that raise legal concerns.

10.3 Managing Up with Difficult Bosses

Managing upward relationships becomes exponentially more challenging when your supervisor has personality disorder traits because traditional approaches often backfire, escalate conflicts, or result in retaliation. Success requires understanding your supervisor's psychological patterns while protecting your career and well-being through strategic communication and boundary management.

Power dynamics shift significantly when personality disorders are involved because these conditions affect judgment, emotional regulation, and interpersonal relationships in ways that can make supervision erratic, unfair, or harmful. Understanding these dynamics helps you develop realistic expectations and appropriate strategies.

Information management becomes crucial because personality-disordered supervisors may use information against you, share confidential details inappropriately, or misinterpret your communications in ways that create problems. This requires careful consideration of what information to share, how to frame communications, and when to seek witnesses or documentation for important interactions.

Expectation setting with personality-disordered supervisors requires extra clarity and frequent confirmation because these individuals may have unrealistic expectations, change requirements unpredictably, or interpret normal workplace interactions in distorted ways. Getting expectations in writing and confirming understanding through email or witnesses provides protection against later disputes.

Feedback navigation proves particularly challenging because personality-disordered supervisors often can't provide fair, constructive feedback due to their own psychological limitations. They may be hypercritical, inconsistent, or unable to separate personal reactions from professional evaluation. Learning to extract useful information while protecting your self-esteem requires sophisticated emotional regulation skills.

Conflict management with supervisors who have personality disorders requires different strategies than normal workplace disagreements because these individuals may escalate conflicts irrationally, hold grudges disproportionately, or retaliate against perceived slights. Prevention often proves more effective than resolution once conflicts have begun.

Lisa, a financial analyst, learned to manage up effectively with Robert, whose paranoid traits made him suspicious of colleagues' motives and resistant to normal collaboration. Lisa adapted her communication style to address his concerns proactively: she provided extra detail about her work processes, shared preliminary results before final reports, and included explicit explanations for her analytical choices. She scheduled regular check-ins to provide updates and address concerns before they escalated into suspicions. When Robert questioned her methodology or motives, she responded with additional documentation and transparent explanations rather than becoming defensive. She also built relationships with Robert's supervisor and peers to provide alternative perspectives on her work quality and professional conduct. This approach helped her maintain a productive working relationship while protecting her professional reputation from Robert's distorted perceptions.

Alliance building involves developing relationships with your supervisor's peers, other departments, or senior management that provide alternative perspectives on your performance and professional value. These relationships can provide protection against unfair treatment while offering career development opportunities beyond your immediate reporting relationship.

Performance documentation becomes especially important when working for personality-disordered supervisors who may provide unfair evaluations, inconsistent feedback, or retaliatory performance assessments. Maintaining your own records of accomplishments, positive feedback from colleagues, and objective performance metrics provides protection against distorted evaluations.

Exit strategy development may be necessary when personality-disordered supervisors create unsustainable working conditions that affect your health, career development, or professional reputation. Having clear plans for internal transfers, external opportunities, or escalation procedures provides options when situations become untenable.

10.4 Navigating Office Politics and Alliances

Office politics become more complex and potentially dangerous when personality-disordered individuals are involved because they often manipulate relationships, create false alliances, and use interpersonal drama to advance their own interests while harming others' reputations and careers. Successfully navigating these dynamics requires understanding manipulation tactics while maintaining your own integrity and professional relationships.

Political awareness involves understanding how personality disorders affect workplace dynamics, who has real versus perceived power, and which relationships are genuine versus manipulative. This awareness helps you make informed decisions about alliances, information sharing, and strategic positioning within your organization.

Alliance evaluation requires assessing whether relationships are based on mutual professional respect and shared goals or manipulation and exploitation. Healthy alliances provide mutual benefit, honest communication, and support during challenges. Manipulative alliances involve one-sided benefit, information exploitation, or attempts to recruit you against other colleagues.

Information warfare represents one of the most dangerous aspects of personality disorder office politics because these individuals often share confidential information, spread rumors, or use personal details against colleagues. Protecting yourself requires controlling information flow while avoiding participation in gossip or manipulation attempts.

Triangulation avoidance involves refusing to participate when personality-disordered individuals try to create conflicts between other people, share inappropriate information about colleagues, or recruit allies for interpersonal battles. Maintaining direct communication and declining to serve as messenger or mediator protects you from manipulation while preserving professional relationships.

Reputation protection requires active management of your professional image and relationships because personality-disordered individuals may attempt to damage your reputation through false accusations, rumor spreading, or manipulation of performance evaluations. Building strong relationships based on demonstrated competence provides protection against character assassination attempts.

David, a software engineer, navigated complex office politics created by Marcus, whose narcissistic traits led him to create competing factions within the development team. Marcus would share confidential information about some colleagues with others, attempt to recruit allies against team members he perceived as threats, and manipulate project assignments to advance his own status. David protected himself by maintaining direct relationships with all team members, declining to participate in gossip or complaints about colleagues, and focusing conversations on work-related topics rather than personal opinions about other people. When Marcus attempted to share negative information about colleagues, David responded with neutral statements like "I prefer to form my own opinions based on direct experience" and redirected conversations to project topics. He also built relationships with managers and colleagues outside his immediate team to provide broader perspective on his work quality and professional conduct.

Neutral positioning involves maintaining professional relationships with all colleagues while avoiding taking sides in personality disorder-created conflicts. This neutrality protects you from retaliation while preserving your ability to work effectively with all team members regardless of interpersonal drama.

Strategic transparency means being open about your work, decisions, and professional conduct while maintaining appropriate privacy about personal matters. This transparency protects against false accusations while demonstrating integrity and professionalism that builds trust with colleagues and supervisors.

Documentation value of political interactions includes recording attempts to manipulate you, pressure you into inappropriate actions, or involve you in conflicts with other colleagues. This documentation can provide protection if false accusations arise or if patterns of manipulation need to be reported to management.

10.5 Exit Conversations and Reference Management

Exit conversations and reference management require special consideration when leaving situations involving personality-disordered colleagues because these individuals may attempt to interfere with your departure, damage your references, or create problems during transition periods. Strategic planning for these conversations protects your reputation while ensuring smooth professional transitions.

Exit conversation preparation involves planning what information to share, how to frame your departure reasons, and which individuals to inform directly versus through official channels. The goal is to maintain professionalism while avoiding manipulation or retaliation attempts during your departure process.

Reason framing should focus on positive opportunities rather than negative experiences when discussing your departure with colleagues or supervisors. Even if personality disorder impacts contributed significantly to your decision, framing your departure in terms of career advancement, new challenges, or professional growth protects your reputation while avoiding conflicts during transition periods.

Information control during exit conversations involves sharing appropriate professional information while protecting confidential details about your new position, future plans, or opinions about current workplace dynamics. Personality-disordered individuals may try to extract information they can use manipulatively or share inappropriately with others.

Reference strategy requires identifying colleagues who can provide accurate, positive references based on direct knowledge of your work quality and professional conduct. These relationships should be cultivated throughout your employment rather than only during departure periods, and should include individuals who are relatively protected from personality disorder manipulation.

Reference protection involves providing context to reference contacts about potential interference or false information they might receive from personality-disordered colleagues. This doesn't mean sharing diagnostic information or personal opinions, but rather preparing references for possible attempts to damage your reputation.

Jennifer, a project manager, strategically managed her exit from a position where Patricia's histrionic traits had created ongoing workplace drama and interpersonal conflicts. Jennifer identified three colleagues who had direct knowledge of her work quality and were relatively protected from Patricia's manipulation attempts. She prepared these references by scheduling individual meetings to discuss her departure and express appreciation for their support, without discussing Patricia's behavior or workplace conflicts. She framed her departure as an exciting career advancement opportunity rather than an escape from difficult circumstances. When Patricia attempted to extract information about Jennifer's new position and salary, Jennifer responded with minimal details: "I'm excited about the new opportunity" and redirected conversations to transition planning topics. She documented any attempts at interference or inappropriate information requests to protect against potential future problems.

Transition professionalism involves completing your responsibilities thoroughly, providing appropriate documentation for your successor, and maintaining positive relationships despite any personality disorder challenges you've experienced. This professionalism protects your reputation while ensuring smooth organizational transitions.

Legal considerations may include non-disclosure agreements, non-compete clauses, or other employment contract provisions that affect what information you can share about your departure or future plans.

Understanding these legal obligations helps you navigate exit conversations appropriately while protecting your interests.

Follow-up protocols establish appropriate boundaries for post-employment contact while maintaining valuable professional relationships. This might include periodic updates with trusted colleagues while declining inappropriate contact attempts from personality-disordered individuals who may seek continued drama or information after your departure.

Network maintenance ensures your professional relationships continue benefiting your career development while protecting against manipulation or interference from former colleagues with personality disorders. This requires ongoing attention to relationship quality and appropriate boundaries that serve your long-term professional interests.

Communication as Armor

Strategic communication with personality-disordered colleagues transforms your interpersonal interactions from potential battlegrounds into managed professional exchanges that serve your career while protecting your well-being. These techniques aren't about becoming manipulative yourself but rather about adapting your communication style to achieve productive outcomes in challenging interpersonal environments.

The skills presented here serve broader professional purposes beyond managing personality disorder challenges. Learning to communicate strategically, manage difficult conversations, and protect your professional reputation through documentation and relationship management are capabilities that benefit any career in any organization.

Most importantly, these communication strategies preserve your ability to remain compassionate and professional while protecting yourself from psychological harm. You don't have to choose between being a good person and protecting yourself—strategic communication allows you to maintain your values while reducing your exposure to manipulation, emotional volatility, and interpersonal drama.

Mastering these techniques takes practice and patience, but the investment pays dividends in reduced workplace stress, improved professional relationships, and greater confidence in your ability to handle challenging interpersonal situations. These skills become part of your permanent professional toolkit that serves you throughout your career regardless of the specific challenges you may face.

The goal isn't to become guarded or defensive in all your workplace relationships but to have the skills necessary to adapt your communication style when circumstances require protection while maintaining effectiveness and professionalism in all your interactions.

Strategic Communication Essentials:

- Gray Rock techniques provide protection from attention-seeking and drama-creating personality types by making yourself uninteresting as a target for manipulation
- Email strategies create documentation while allowing thoughtful responses that protect against impulsive reactions and emotional escalation
- Managing up with personality-disordered supervisors requires understanding power dynamics while protecting your career through strategic information management
- Office politics navigation involves avoiding manipulation while maintaining professional relationships and protecting your reputation from false accusations
- Exit conversations and reference management require planning to protect your professional reputation while ensuring smooth transitions away from challenging situations
- Strategic communication preserves your ability to remain professional and compassionate while protecting yourself from psychological harm and career damage

Chapter 11: The Stay-or-Go Decision Framework

The ship's captain doesn't abandon vessel at the first sign of rough weather, but neither does she ignore gathering storm clouds that signal conditions too dangerous to navigate safely. Similarly, deciding to remain in a workplace with personality-disordered colleagues requires careful assessment of multiple factors: your ability to protect yourself, the organization's willingness to address problems, the impact on your health and career, and the availability of better alternatives.

This decision framework helps you evaluate your situation systematically rather than making choices based purely on emotion, frustration, or fear. Sometimes staying and implementing protective strategies proves most beneficial for your career and well-being. Other times, departure becomes necessary to preserve your health, advance your career, or escape situations that have become professionally or personally unsustainable.

11.1 The STOP Method for Decision Making

The STOP method provides a structured approach for evaluating whether to remain in challenging workplace situations or seek alternatives elsewhere. This framework helps you assess your situation objectively while considering both immediate circumstances and long-term implications for your career and well-being.

S - Situation Assessment involves objectively evaluating your current workplace conditions, including the severity and frequency of personality disorder impacts, organizational responses to problems, available support resources, and your ability to implement protective strategies effectively. This assessment requires honest reflection about what's actually happening versus what you hoped would happen.

T - Threshold Analysis determines your personal limits for acceptable workplace stress, interpersonal conflict, and professional development opportunities. Everyone's threshold differs based on their career stage, financial situation, family obligations, and personal resilience. Understanding your limits helps you make decisions that align with your values and circumstances.

O - Options Evaluation explores all available alternatives, including staying with modified strategies, requesting transfers within your organization, seeking external opportunities, or pursuing formal interventions through HR or legal channels. Thorough options evaluation prevents premature decisions while ensuring you don't miss potentially beneficial alternatives.

P - Plan Development creates specific strategies for your chosen course of action, including timelines, resource requirements, risk mitigation measures, and success indicators. Planning transforms decision-making from wishful thinking into actionable strategies that increase your likelihood of positive outcomes.

Situation assessment criteria include the frequency and severity of personality disorder incidents, organizational willingness to address problems, availability of protective resources, impact on your work quality and career development, effects on your physical and mental health, and influence on your relationships outside work.

Threshold factors encompass your financial flexibility, career advancement opportunities, professional development needs, family considerations, health impacts, and personal values about workplace relationships and professional contribution. Understanding these factors helps you make decisions that align with your broader life goals rather than just immediate frustrations.

Options analysis requires researching internal transfer possibilities, external job market conditions, professional development alternatives, legal protection options, and support resources that might improve your current situation. Comprehensive analysis often reveals options that weren't initially apparent while preventing decisions based on incomplete information.

Sarah, a marketing manager, used the STOP method to evaluate her situation working with David, whose antisocial traits had created ongoing ethical concerns and interpersonal conflicts. Her situation assessment revealed that David's behavior was escalating despite organizational interventions, affecting her team's productivity and her own job satisfaction significantly. Her threshold analysis indicated that the stress was affecting her health and relationships outside work beyond acceptable levels. Her options evaluation revealed internal transfer possibilities to other marketing roles, external opportunities in her geographic area, and potential for formal intervention through legal consultation. She developed a plan that included applying for internal transfers while simultaneously exploring external opportunities and consulting with an employment attorney about David's increasingly concerning behavior. This systematic approach helped her make decisions based on comprehensive analysis rather than emotional reactions to daily workplace stress.

Decision timing considerations include organizational changes that might improve or worsen conditions, personal circumstances that affect your flexibility, job market conditions that influence external opportunities, and seasonal factors that impact transition planning. Strategic timing can significantly improve outcomes regardless of which decision you make.

Contingency planning prepares you for different scenarios and unexpected developments that might affect your chosen course of action. This includes backup plans if your preferred option doesn't work out, strategies for managing transition periods, and resources for dealing with potential retaliation or complications during implementation.

11.2 Financial and Career Planning Considerations

Financial security and career trajectory planning become crucial factors in stay-or-go decisions because they affect your ability to take risks, negotiate from positions of strength, and make choices that serve your long-term interests rather than just immediate relief from workplace stress.

Financial assessment includes evaluating your emergency fund adequacy, monthly expense requirements, benefits comparison between current and potential positions, severance or transition compensation possibilities, and costs associated with job searching or career transitions. Financial security provides options that financial stress eliminates.

Career trajectory analysis examines how your current position serves your professional development goals, skill building requirements, industry experience needs, and networking opportunities. Sometimes staying in challenging situations provides career advancement that compensates for interpersonal difficulties, while other times leaving becomes necessary to prevent career stagnation or damage.

Benefits evaluation encompasses health insurance coverage, retirement contributions, vacation accrual, professional development funding, and other compensation elements that affect your total employment value. Benefits packages often represent significant value that must be factored into stay-or-go calculations.

Transition costs include job search expenses, potential relocation costs, temporary income reduction, COBRA health insurance premiums, and opportunity costs of time spent searching rather than working. Understanding these costs helps you plan realistic timelines and resource allocation for potential transitions.

Market research involves analyzing salary ranges for your skills and experience, demand for your expertise in your geographic area, industry trends that might affect opportunities, and networking requirements for accessing better positions. Market knowledge helps you evaluate whether external opportunities offer genuine improvements over current situations.

Michael, a software developer, conducted thorough financial and career planning before deciding to leave his position due to ongoing conflicts with Jennifer, whose borderline traits had created a toxic team environment. His financial assessment revealed six months of emergency savings, minimal debt obligations, and benefits that could be replaced through new employment or COBRA coverage. His career analysis showed that staying would limit his professional development due to team dysfunction, while leaving could provide opportunities for advancement and skill building in healthier environments. He researched market conditions and discovered strong demand for his technical skills, competitive salary ranges above his current compensation, and multiple companies with positive workplace cultures. This analysis supported his decision to leave while providing realistic expectations about transition timelines and financial requirements.

Income replacement strategies might include consulting work during transition periods, part-time employment while searching for full-time positions, freelance projects that maintain cash flow, or temporary positions that provide flexibility during job searches. Having multiple income options reduces financial pressure while expanding your negotiation flexibility.

Career protection measures ensure that difficult workplace situations don't damage your professional reputation, skill development, or industry relationships in ways that affect future opportunities. This might include building external professional networks, maintaining current certifications and skills, or documenting achievements that demonstrate your capabilities despite workplace challenges.

Long-term planning considers how current decisions affect your career prospects five or ten years from now, retirement planning implications, professional development trajectories, and geographic flexibility that might influence future opportunities. Short-term relief from workplace stress shouldn't compromise long-term career and financial goals.

11.3 Building Your Exit Strategy

Exit strategy development provides security and confidence whether you ultimately decide to stay or leave because knowing you have viable alternatives reduces anxiety while improving your negotiation position and decision-making clarity. Effective exit strategies require careful planning, relationship management, and resource development.

Timeline development includes realistic job search duration estimates, notice period requirements, project completion obligations, and personal readiness factors that affect transition timing. Rushed exits often create unnecessary complications while overly delayed departures may compromise your well-being or opportunities.

Skill inventory assesses your current marketability, identifies development needs that improve your attractiveness to potential employers, and creates improvement plans that can be implemented while still employed. Strong skills and qualifications provide confidence and options during transition planning.

Network activation involves reconnecting with professional contacts, building relationships with industry colleagues, engaging with recruiters in your field, and participating in professional organizations that provide job search resources and opportunities. Networks often provide access to opportunities that aren't publicly advertised.

Portfolio development includes updating your resume with recent achievements, gathering references from trusted colleagues, creating work samples that demonstrate your capabilities, and building online profiles that represent your professional brand effectively. Strong portfolios reduce job search timelines while improving offer quality.

Interview preparation covers common questions about leaving current positions, explanations for employment gaps or transitions, demonstration of skills and experience relevant to target positions, and questions about organizational culture and workplace dynamics that help you avoid similar problems in future positions.

Lisa, an HR specialist, spent six months building her exit strategy while managing ongoing challenges created by Marcus, whose narcissistic traits had made her work environment increasingly difficult. She updated her certifications through online courses, rebuilt her professional network by attending industry conferences and joining HR associations, updated her resume with specific achievements and metrics from her current role, and cultivated references from colleagues who could speak to her professional capabilities. She researched target companies thoroughly, including employee reviews and workplace culture assessments, to avoid similar personality disorder challenges in future positions. She practiced interview responses that framed her departure positively while addressing potential concerns about her reasons for leaving. This preparation enabled her to secure a better position with improved compensation and workplace culture when she decided to leave.

Reference cultivation requires building relationships with colleagues who can provide strong recommendations based on direct knowledge of your work quality and professional conduct. These relationships should be developed throughout your employment rather than only during departure planning, and should include individuals who are relatively protected from personality disorder manipulation.

Legal protection involves understanding your employment contract obligations, non-compete or non-disclosure requirements, intellectual property considerations, and potential severance or transition benefits. Legal knowledge protects you from complications while ensuring you maximize available benefits and protections.

Reputation management ensures your departure maintains positive professional relationships while protecting against potential retaliation or reputation damage from personality-disordered colleagues. This includes careful communication about departure plans, professional conduct during transition periods, and ongoing relationship maintenance that serves your long-term career interests.

11.4 Protecting References and Reputation

Reference and reputation protection requires proactive management because personality-disordered individuals may attempt to interfere with your job search, damage your professional relationships, or provide false information to potential employers. Strategic planning prevents these interferences while ensuring you have strong advocates for your professional capabilities.

Reference selection focuses on colleagues who have direct knowledge of your work quality, are relatively protected from personality disorder manipulation, understand professional reference requirements, and can provide specific examples of your capabilities and achievements. Quality references often matter more than quantity in competitive job markets.

Reference preparation involves providing references with information about positions you're seeking, specific skills or experiences that should be highlighted, potential concerns that might be raised, and context about your current workplace situation without inappropriate disclosure of personal information about colleagues.

Information management controls what information is shared about your job search, departure plans, and new opportunities to prevent interference or manipulation by personality-disordered colleagues. This includes careful timing of announcements, selective disclosure to trusted colleagues, and protection of confidential details about potential employers.

Damage prevention involves anticipating potential interference attempts and developing strategies to prevent or address them effectively. This might include warning references about possible false information, building relationships with multiple potential references, or documenting your work quality and professional conduct to counter false accusations.

Reputation monitoring includes staying aware of what information is being shared about you within your organization, addressing false rumors or accusations promptly, and maintaining positive relationships that provide accurate information about your professional capabilities and conduct.

David, a project manager, protected his references and reputation while leaving a position where Patricia's histrionic traits had created ongoing interpersonal drama that threatened to affect his professional standing. He identified five colleagues from different departments who had direct knowledge of his project management capabilities and were relatively insulated from Patricia's manipulation attempts. He prepared these references by scheduling individual meetings to discuss his departure, providing information about the types of positions he was seeking, and expressing appreciation for their support without discussing workplace conflicts or personality issues. He managed information carefully by informing only trusted colleagues about his job search timeline and keeping details about potential opportunities confidential until formal offers were received. He monitored his professional reputation by maintaining relationships with colleagues who could provide accurate information about workplace dynamics and his professional conduct.

Documentation value for reputation protection includes performance evaluations, project success records, client feedback, colleague testimonials, and achievement documentation that provides objective evidence of your professional capabilities. This documentation counters potential false information while supporting positive references.

Professional networking builds relationships outside your current organization that provide alternative perspectives on your capabilities while reducing dependence on current workplace references. Industry contacts, former colleagues, and professional association relationships often provide valuable references and opportunities.

Legal considerations may include defamation protection if false information is being spread about your professional conduct, employment law requirements about reference information, and documentation that supports your version of workplace events if disputes arise about your performance or conduct.

11.5 Recovery and Moving Forward

Recovery from challenging workplace experiences involving personality-disordered colleagues requires intentional effort to process experiences, rebuild confidence, develop improved skills, and create strategies for avoiding similar problems in future positions. This recovery process serves both healing and prevention purposes while strengthening your overall professional resilience.

Emotional processing involves acknowledging the impact that personality disorder workplace challenges have had on your confidence, stress levels, professional relationships, and overall well-being. Processing these impacts helps you identify areas needing attention while preventing unresolved issues from affecting future workplace relationships.

Skill development includes building capabilities that were tested during your challenging workplace experience, such as boundary setting, conflict management, communication strategies, and stress resilience. These enhanced skills prepare you for future leadership roles while improving your overall professional effectiveness.

Confidence rebuilding focuses on reconnecting with your professional strengths, achievements, and capabilities that may have been undermined by personality disorder workplace dynamics. This includes celebrating successes, acknowledging your resilience in managing difficult situations, and developing realistic assessments of your professional value.

Pattern recognition helps you identify warning signs of similar workplace problems in future positions while developing strategies for addressing them early before they become major issues. Learning from experience improves your ability to make better workplace decisions and protect yourself proactively.

Future prevention involves developing interview questions that assess workplace culture, relationship management skills that help you build positive professional networks, and early warning systems that help you recognize personality disorder impacts before they become overwhelming.

Jennifer, a financial analyst, focused on recovery and future prevention after successfully transitioning away from a position where Robert's paranoid traits had created ongoing stress and professional challenges. She worked with a career coach to process her experience and identify lessons learned about workplace dynamics, professional boundary setting, and stress management. She developed interview questions about team collaboration, conflict resolution, and management styles that helped her assess workplace culture in potential positions. She built her professional network by joining industry associations and reconnecting with former colleagues who provided positive perspectives on her capabilities. She developed early warning systems for recognizing personality disorder impacts and strategies for addressing them before they became overwhelming. Most importantly, she celebrated her resilience in managing difficult circumstances while building a successful career despite interpersonal challenges.

Success integration involves recognizing how you successfully managed challenging circumstances, developed new capabilities, and maintained your professional effectiveness despite difficult interpersonal dynamics. This recognition builds confidence while providing models for handling future challenges.

Support system maintenance ensures you continue benefiting from relationships and resources that helped you manage workplace challenges while building new connections that support your ongoing professional development and personal well-being.

Professional growth uses lessons learned from managing personality disorder workplace challenges to advance your career, improve your leadership capabilities, and contribute to healthier workplace cultures that benefit all employees. Your experience provides valuable perspective for helping others and improving organizational effectiveness.

Long-term perspective frames challenging workplace experiences as temporary situations that contributed to your professional development rather than defining characteristics of your career or personal capabilities. This perspective promotes resilience while preventing bitterness or defensiveness that could limit future opportunities.

Charting Your Course

Making stay-or-go decisions about challenging workplace situations requires the same careful navigation skills that ship captains use to guide vessels through dangerous waters. You must assess current conditions realistically, understand your vessel's capabilities and limitations, evaluate available routes to safety, and make decisions that serve your long-term destination rather than just immediate comfort.

The framework presented here acknowledges that there are no universally right answers to these complex decisions. What works for one person's circumstances, career stage, and personal situation may be inappropriate for another's. The goal isn't to provide simple formulas but to give you tools for making informed decisions that align with your values, serve your interests, and protect your well-being.

Sometimes staying and implementing protective strategies proves most beneficial for your career development, financial security, and professional growth. Other times leaving becomes necessary to preserve your health, advance your career, or escape situations that have become unsustainable despite your best efforts to manage them effectively.

Whatever decision you make, the skills you've developed managing personality disorder workplace challenges—boundary setting, strategic communication, documentation, networking, and resilience building—will serve you throughout your career. These capabilities prepare you for leadership roles, improve your overall professional effectiveness, and help you contribute to healthier workplace cultures wherever your career takes you.

Most importantly, trust your judgment and value your well-being. You deserve to work in environments that allow you to thrive professionally while maintaining your health and happiness. The decision-making framework provides structure for your choices, but ultimately you must chart the course that serves your unique circumstances and aspirations.

Decision-Making Framework:

- The STOP method provides systematic evaluation of situation, thresholds, options, and plans for making informed stay-or-go decisions
- Financial and career planning considerations ensure decisions serve long-term interests rather than just immediate relief from workplace stress
- Exit strategy development provides security and options whether you ultimately decide to stay or leave your current position
- Reference and reputation protection prevents personality-disordered colleagues from interfering with your career transitions and professional opportunities
- Recovery and moving forward involves processing experiences while building skills and strategies that prevent similar problems in future positions
- Successful decision-making requires trusting your judgment while using systematic frameworks to evaluate complex workplace situations objectively

Chapter 12: Hiring and Screening Best Practices

The master chef doesn't discover that their main ingredient is spoiled after they've spent hours preparing an elaborate meal—they inspect everything carefully before cooking begins. Similarly, the most effective strategy for managing personality disorders in the workplace involves preventing problematic hires rather than trying to fix situations after dysfunction has already taken root in your organization.

Hiring decisions create the foundation for all future workplace dynamics, team effectiveness, and organizational culture. When you hire individuals with untreated personality disorders who aren't suited for your work environment, you're not just adding one problematic employee—you're potentially disrupting entire teams, damaging productivity, and creating legal and safety risks that can persist for years. Smart screening practices protect your organization while ensuring you build teams that can thrive together.

12.1 Legal Considerations in Personality Screening

Employment law creates both opportunities and constraints for personality screening during hiring processes. You can assess behavioral patterns, work history, and interpersonal skills that indicate personality disorder traits, but you cannot discriminate based on disability status or ask direct questions about mental health conditions. Understanding these legal boundaries helps you screen effectively while protecting your organization from discrimination claims.

Protected class limitations prevent direct questions about mental health history, personality disorder diagnoses, or psychiatric treatment. You cannot ask candidates if they've been diagnosed with personality disorders, received mental health treatment, or have conditions that might affect their work performance. These protections exist to prevent discrimination against individuals with mental health conditions.

Behavioral assessment permissions allow you to evaluate how candidates handle workplace situations, interact with others, respond to stress, and manage professional relationships. You can ask about specific behaviors, work conflicts, and problem-solving approaches that reveal personality patterns without directly addressing mental health status.

Job-related screening focuses on essential functions and requirements that legitimate business needs require. If teamwork is essential for a position, you can assess collaborative skills extensively. If customer service requires emotional regulation, you can evaluate stress management and interpersonal capabilities. The key is connecting screening questions to actual job requirements rather than general personality preferences.

Documentation requirements protect your hiring decisions from later discrimination claims by showing that selections were based on job-related qualifications rather than protected characteristics. This includes recording specific behavioral observations, comparing candidates using consistent criteria, and maintaining objective evaluation records.

Sarah, an HR director at a technology consulting firm, developed legal screening practices after experiencing problems with several hires whose personality traits had created ongoing team conflicts. She worked with employment attorneys to create interview protocols that assessed collaboration skills, conflict resolution abilities, and stress management without asking about mental health history. Her questions included "Describe a time when you disagreed with a team member about project direction. How did you handle the situation?" and "Tell me about a high-pressure deadline situation. What strategies did you use to manage your own stress while supporting your teammates?" These questions revealed personality patterns while staying within legal boundaries. When candidates demonstrated concerning responses—such as blaming others entirely for conflicts or describing aggressive responses to stress—she documented specific examples and used consistent evaluation criteria to make hiring decisions.

Accommodation considerations require understanding that some personality disorder traits might be protected disabilities requiring reasonable accommodation. This means you cannot automatically exclude candidates who might need workplace accommodations, but you can assess their ability to perform essential job functions with or without reasonable accommodation.

Reference check legalities allow you to ask former employers about work performance, interpersonal relationships, and behavioral patterns that affected job effectiveness. However, you cannot ask references to disclose mental health information or provide opinions about candidates' psychological conditions. Focus on observable behaviors and work-related impacts.

Pre-employment testing limitations restrict what psychological assessments you can use during hiring processes. General personality tests that aren't directly job-related may violate ADA requirements, while assessments that reveal mental health conditions are generally prohibited. However, you can use behavioral assessments that measure job-relevant skills and capabilities.

Interview consistency requires asking all candidates similar questions and using comparable evaluation criteria to avoid claims of discriminatory treatment. This doesn't mean asking identical questions but rather ensuring that your assessment process treats all candidates fairly while evaluating job-relevant qualifications consistently.

12.2 Behavioral Interview Techniques

Behavioral interviewing reveals how candidates actually behave in workplace situations rather than how they think they should behave or what they believe interviewers want to hear. This technique proves particularly effective for identifying personality disorder traits because these conditions involve consistent behavioral patterns that emerge across different situations and relationships.

STAR methodology structures behavioral questions to elicit specific examples: Situation (context for the story), Task (what needed to be accomplished), Action (what the candidate actually did), and Result (what happened because of their actions). This framework prevents vague responses while revealing actual behavioral patterns.

Conflict resolution assessment explores how candidates handle disagreements, criticism, and interpersonal tension. Personality disorders often become apparent in how individuals respond to conflict situations. Ask questions like "Describe a time when you strongly disagreed with your supervisor's decision. How did you handle it?" or "Tell me about a situation where a colleague criticized your work. What was your response?"

Team collaboration evaluation reveals how candidates work with others, share credit, and handle group dynamics. Questions might include "Give me an example of a team project that didn't go as planned. What was your role in addressing the problems?" or "Describe a time when you had to work closely with someone whose work style was very different from yours."

Stress response analysis shows how candidates manage pressure, deadlines, and challenging situations. Ask "Tell me about the most stressful work situation you've experienced. How did you handle it?" or "Describe a time when you made a significant mistake at work. What did you do about it?"

Leadership and authority assessment explores how candidates interact with supervisors, exercise authority over others, and handle power dynamics. Questions include "Describe your relationship with the best boss you've ever had. What made it work so well?" or "Tell me about a time when you had to give difficult feedback to a colleague or subordinate."

Michael, a department manager, used behavioral interviewing to screen candidates for a customer service role after experiencing problems with a previous hire whose borderline traits had created emotional volatility and customer complaints. His questions included "Describe a time when a customer became extremely upset with you personally. How did you handle the situation and your own emotional response?" One candidate described screaming back at an angry customer and then crying in the bathroom afterward, revealing emotional volatility that would be problematic in customer service. Another candidate described staying calm, empathizing with the customer's frustration, and working systematically to resolve the issue while seeking supervisor support when needed. These responses revealed significantly different emotional regulation capabilities that directly related to job performance requirements.

Response evaluation criteria help you identify concerning patterns versus normal workplace challenges. Red flags include blaming others exclusively for problems, showing no empathy for other perspectives, describing manipulative or dishonest solutions, expressing grandiose self-assessment, or demonstrating emotional volatility in their storytelling.

Follow-up questioning probes deeper into concerning responses to understand patterns rather than isolated incidents. If a candidate mentions conflict with multiple supervisors, ask "What patterns do you notice in these situations?" If they describe taking credit for team success, ask "What role did your teammates play in that achievement?"

Non-verbal assessment observes body language, emotional reactions, and interpersonal style during interviews. Notice if candidates become defensive when asked about conflicts, show inappropriate emotional intensity, or demonstrate poor social awareness through their interview behavior.

Scenario-based questions present hypothetical workplace situations to evaluate judgment and decision-making. For example, "If you discovered a colleague was sharing confidential client information inappropriately, what would you do?" or "How would you handle a situation where your teammates consistently missed deadlines that affected your ability to complete your work?"

12.3 Reference Checking for Character

Reference checking provides opportunities to verify candidates' behavioral patterns and interpersonal effectiveness through the experiences of people who've worked with them directly. However, many organizations conduct superficial reference checks that miss personality disorder red flags because they don't ask the right questions or probe deeply enough into behavioral patterns.

Strategic reference selection involves talking to people who've observed the candidate in different roles and relationships. Include direct supervisors, peers, and subordinates when possible. Former colleagues often provide more honest assessments than current ones who might worry about workplace relationships or confidentiality concerns.

Behavioral focus questions ask references to describe specific examples rather than general impressions. Instead of "Was she a good team player?" ask "Can you give me an example of how she handled a situation where team members disagreed about project direction?" Instead of "How did he manage stress?" ask "Describe a high-pressure situation you observed him handle."

Pattern identification involves asking about consistency across time and situations. Questions like "How did his work relationships change over the time you worked together?" or "Did you notice any patterns in how she responded to feedback or criticism?" can reveal personality disorder progression that might not be apparent in single examples.

Interpersonal assessment explores how candidates affected workplace relationships and team dynamics. Ask "How did other team members respond to working with her?" or "Did you notice any changes in team dynamics when he joined or left the group?"

Problem exploration directly asks about difficulties or challenges without being accusatory. Questions like "What advice would you give him for continued professional development?" or "Were there any situations where you had to provide extra coaching or support?" can reveal areas of concern.

Jennifer, an operations manager, developed thorough reference checking after hiring David, whose antisocial traits hadn't been apparent during interviews but created ongoing ethical violations and team disruption. For subsequent hires, she asked references specific questions: "Can you describe a time when this person had to admit they made a mistake? How did they handle it?" One reference revealed that a candidate had never acknowledged errors despite several significant problems, instead blaming colleagues and circumstances consistently. Another reference described how a different candidate had appropriated a colleague's innovative idea and presented it as his own to senior management. These behavioral patterns indicated personality traits that would be problematic in collaborative work environments.

Reference honesty indicators help you assess whether references are providing candid feedback or trying to avoid saying anything negative. Listen for overly generic praise, hesitation when asked for specific examples, focus on technical skills while avoiding interpersonal topics, or suggestions that candidates might be "better suited for different environments."

Legal boundaries for reference questions focus on job performance and observable behaviors rather than personal characteristics or protected information. You can ask about work quality, teamwork, reliability, and professional conduct, but you cannot ask about mental health, personal relationships, or other protected areas.

Documentation practices record reference responses objectively, noting specific examples and behavioral descriptions they provide. This documentation supports hiring decisions while providing protection against discrimination claims. Focus on factual information rather than interpretive judgments about personality or character.

Red flag patterns in references include multiple former employers who are unwilling to provide detailed feedback, references who redirect questions about interpersonal relationships to technical skills, patterns of short employment duration with different organizations, or references who provide specific examples of concerning behaviors but frame them as misunderstandings or personality conflicts.

12.4 Probationary Period Management

Probationary periods provide structured opportunities to evaluate new hires' actual workplace behavior while maintaining flexibility to address problems before they become entrenched. Many personality disorder traits that don't appear during interviews become apparent within the first few months of employment, making effective probationary management essential for preventing long-term problems.

Structured evaluation involves setting clear expectations, monitoring specific behaviors, documenting observations, and providing regular feedback throughout the probationary period. This structure protects both employees and employers while ensuring fair evaluation of actual workplace performance.

Behavioral monitoring focuses on interpersonal relationships, team collaboration, conflict resolution, response to feedback, and adaptation to workplace culture. These areas often reveal personality disorder traits that technical skills assessment might miss during initial hiring processes.

Documentation requirements include specific behavioral examples, dates and circumstances, witness information when relevant, and clear connections between observations and job performance requirements. Good documentation supports personnel decisions while providing protection against legal challenges.

Feedback systems provide regular check-ins that allow course correction for minor issues while identifying major personality or behavioral problems that require more significant intervention.

Weekly or bi-weekly meetings during probationary periods help identify problems early while demonstrating organizational commitment to employee success.

Performance standards should be clearly defined and consistently applied to all probationary employees. This includes technical job requirements as well as behavioral expectations for teamwork, communication, professional conduct, and workplace relationships.

Lisa, a team leader in a marketing agency, used structured probationary management after hiring Robert, whose interview had seemed promising but whose paranoid traits began creating team tension within weeks. Her probationary evaluation included weekly one-on-one meetings, monthly team feedback sessions, and documentation of specific behavioral incidents. During the second week, Robert accused colleagues of monitoring his computer usage and undermining his project contributions. Lisa documented these concerns objectively while providing clear explanations of normal workplace practices. By the sixth week, Robert's suspicions had escalated to include beliefs that clients were conspiring against him and colleagues were stealing his ideas. Lisa's documentation showed a clear pattern of paranoid thinking that was affecting team relationships and project effectiveness, supporting her decision to terminate during the probationary period before these patterns became more entrenched or legally protected.

Team integration assessment evaluates how new hires affect existing team dynamics, whether they build positive relationships with colleagues, and how other team members respond to working with them. This assessment often reveals personality disorder impacts that individual performance reviews might miss.

Intervention opportunities during probationary periods include coaching for minor behavioral issues, clarification of expectations and workplace norms, connection with employee assistance resources, and modification of assignments or work environment when appropriate. However, intervention should be balanced with realistic assessment of whether personality-related problems are likely to improve with time and support.

Legal considerations ensure that probationary evaluations follow consistent procedures, focus on job-related performance, and provide appropriate accommodation discussions if mental health factors become apparent. Probationary terminations should be based on legitimate performance concerns rather than personality characteristics or protected conditions.

Decision criteria for probationary period conclusions include technical job performance, behavioral standards compliance, team relationship effectiveness, adaptability to workplace culture, and potential for continued improvement with normal supervision and support. Clear criteria help ensure fair evaluation while protecting organizational interests.

12.5 Early Intervention During Onboarding

Early intervention during onboarding prevents minor personality-related issues from developing into major workplace problems while supporting new employees' successful integration into organizational culture. Effective intervention requires recognizing warning signs, providing appropriate resources, and maintaining realistic expectations about what onboarding can and cannot address.

Warning sign recognition involves monitoring for behavioral patterns that might indicate personality disorder traits or workplace adjustment difficulties. These include excessive emotional reactions to routine feedback, persistent conflicts with multiple colleagues, inappropriate boundary violations, or consistent externalization of responsibility for problems.

Resource connection links new employees with appropriate support systems including employee assistance programs, mentoring relationships, training opportunities, and professional development resources. Early connection with resources prevents problems from escalating while demonstrating organizational commitment to employee success.

Cultural integration helps new employees understand workplace norms, communication expectations, and relationship standards that support their success. This is particularly important for individuals who may struggle with social cues or interpersonal boundaries due to personality traits.

Boundary clarification establishes clear expectations about professional conduct, appropriate workplace relationships, and organizational policies that support healthy workplace culture. Clear boundaries prevent problems while protecting all employees from inappropriate behavior.

Support system development connects new employees with colleagues, supervisors, and organizational resources that provide ongoing guidance and assistance. Strong support systems help individuals succeed while providing early warning systems for emerging problems.

David, an HR specialist, developed early intervention practices after noticing that personality disorder-related problems often became apparent during the first few months of employment but weren't being addressed until they had created significant team disruption. His onboarding process included structured check-ins at two weeks, one month, and three months with new employees and their supervisors. During these meetings, he assessed both individual adjustment and team integration impacts. When Marcus, a new financial analyst, began showing narcissistic patterns including credit-taking, grandiose self-presentation, and dismissive treatment of colleagues, David intervened early. He provided additional coaching about collaborative work expectations, connected Marcus with a senior mentor who could model appropriate professional behavior, and established clear performance metrics that included teamwork components. He also provided team members with guidance about maintaining professional boundaries while working with challenging colleagues. This early intervention helped manage Marcus's impact while providing him with clear expectations and support for appropriate workplace behavior.

Intervention timing affects effectiveness significantly because personality-related problems often escalate gradually if not addressed early. Intervention during the first few weeks proves more effective than waiting for problems to become entrenched in workplace relationships and organizational culture.

Accommodation assessment determines if personality-related difficulties might require workplace accommodations under disability laws while distinguishing between protected conditions and inappropriate behavior. Early assessment prevents discrimination while ensuring that legitimate performance standards are maintained.

Team protection involves supporting existing employees who may be affected by new hires' personality traits while maintaining confidentiality and fairness. This might include additional training, modified team assignments, or enhanced supervision during adjustment periods.

Outcome measurement tracks intervention effectiveness through metrics like team satisfaction, productivity measures, conflict frequency, and individual performance indicators. Regular measurement helps refine intervention approaches while demonstrating their value to organizational leadership.

Professional consultation involves connecting with mental health professionals, employment attorneys, or HR specialists who can provide guidance about complex personality-related situations. Early consultation prevents minor issues from becoming major legal or organizational problems while ensuring appropriate resource utilization.

The Foundation of Excellence

Effective hiring and onboarding practices create the foundation for all future workplace relationships and organizational culture. The time and effort invested in careful screening, structured evaluation, and early intervention pay dividends for years through reduced conflict, improved productivity, and healthier workplace dynamics that benefit everyone in your organization.

The techniques presented here balance legitimate business needs with fairness and legal compliance while recognizing that some personality traits create genuine workplace challenges that require proactive management. The goal isn't to exclude all individuals who might have personality difficulties but to make informed decisions about who can succeed in your specific work environment and what support they might need.

Prevention remains far more effective and less costly than attempting to manage personality disorder problems after they've become entrenched in your workplace. The screening methods, evaluation techniques, and intervention strategies outlined here provide tools for building stronger teams while protecting both individual employees and organizational effectiveness.

Smart hiring practices also protect your existing employees from the stress and disruption that problematic colleagues can create. Your current team members deserve workplace environments where they can thrive professionally while maintaining their well-being and productivity. Careful hiring decisions demonstrate organizational commitment to creating positive workplace cultures that serve everyone's interests.

Most importantly, these practices help you build teams that can achieve exceptional results through effective collaboration, mutual respect, and shared commitment to organizational success. When you hire well and support new employees effectively, you create workplace environments where human potential can flourish and organizational goals can be achieved through positive relationships and collective effort.

Essential Hiring Strategies:

- Legal screening practices focus on job-related behaviors and skills while avoiding direct questions about mental health conditions or protected characteristics
- Behavioral interviewing reveals actual response patterns and interpersonal capabilities that predict workplace effectiveness and cultural fit
- Thorough reference checking uncovers behavioral patterns and relationship impacts that interviews alone cannot reveal adequately
- Structured probationary management provides opportunities to evaluate actual workplace behavior while maintaining flexibility for addressing problems early
- Early intervention during onboarding prevents minor personality-related issues from developing into major workplace disruptions
- Prevention through careful hiring proves far more effective than attempting to manage personality disorder problems after they become entrenched

Chapter 13: Creating Psychologically Safe Workplaces

The architect doesn't wait until after construction is complete to consider whether a building can withstand earthquakes—structural reinforcement gets built into the foundation from the very beginning. Similarly, creating psychologically safe workplaces requires intentional design of organizational systems, leadership practices, and cultural norms that prevent toxic behaviors while supporting all employees' ability to contribute authentically and effectively.

Psychological safety—the shared belief that team members can express ideas, ask questions, admit mistakes, and raise concerns without fear of negative consequences—becomes both more challenging and more important when personality disorders are present in workplace settings. These conditions can undermine trust, create unpredictable emotional dynamics, and make colleagues hesitant to engage openly. However, organizations that successfully build psychological safety despite these challenges often discover that their efforts create resilience that serves them well beyond specific personality disorder situations.

13.1 The Four Pillars of Psychological Safety

Psychological safety rests on four foundational pillars that must be intentionally built and maintained through consistent organizational practices. These pillars—predictable leadership, inclusive culture, learning orientation, and clear accountability—work together to create environments where all employees can thrive while problematic behaviors are addressed effectively before they undermine team effectiveness.

Predictable leadership provides consistent responses, fair treatment, and reliable support that employees can count on regardless of changing circumstances or personality-driven workplace drama. Leaders who remain calm during emotional outbursts, maintain consistent standards despite manipulation attempts, and provide equitable treatment regardless of personal relationships demonstrate the stability that psychological safety requires.

Inclusive culture ensures that all team members feel valued, heard, and respected despite differences in personality, communication style, or individual challenges. This includes creating space for diverse perspectives while maintaining boundaries against behavior that undermines others' ability to contribute effectively. Inclusion means supporting individuals with mental health challenges while protecting the team from dysfunction.

Learning orientation encourages experimentation, values feedback, and treats mistakes as opportunities for growth rather than occasions for blame or punishment. This orientation proves particularly important when personality disorders are present because these conditions often involve defensive reactions to criticism or feedback that can stifle learning and improvement.

Clear accountability maintains standards for behavior and performance while providing support for improvement and appropriate consequences for violations. Accountability systems must address personality disorder impacts fairly while avoiding discrimination against mental health conditions.

The marketing department at a consumer electronics company exemplified these four pillars in action when managing Jennifer, whose borderline traits had previously created emotional volatility and interpersonal drama. Department leader Michael demonstrated predictable leadership by maintaining calm responses to Jennifer's emotional outbursts while consistently enforcing professional behavior standards. He created inclusive culture by acknowledging Jennifer's creative contributions while setting clear boundaries about appropriate workplace communication. He built learning orientation by framing feedback sessions as development opportunities rather than criticism, providing written summaries to reduce Jennifer's abandonment fears. Most importantly, he maintained clear accountability by addressing behavioral issues promptly while connecting Jennifer with employee assistance resources that supported her success. These practices created psychological safety for the entire team while helping Jennifer function more effectively within professional boundaries.

Leadership consistency requires that managers respond to similar situations in similar ways regardless of their personal relationships, emotional reactions, or other individuals' manipulation attempts. This consistency builds trust that fair treatment doesn't depend on personality, politics, or favoritism.

Communication standards establish clear expectations for how team members interact with each other, provide feedback, and address conflicts. These standards must be specific enough to prevent personality disorder impacts while flexible enough to accommodate different communication styles and individual needs.

Support systems provide resources that help all employees succeed while addressing individual challenges appropriately. This includes employee assistance programs, mentoring relationships, professional development opportunities, and mental health resources that support both individual success and team effectiveness.

Cultural norms shape how teams handle mistakes, conflicts, and individual differences in ways that promote psychological safety. These norms must explicitly address how to respond to personality disorder impacts while maintaining respect for all team members.

13.2 Leadership Development and Accountability

Leadership capability determines whether organizations can maintain psychological safety despite personality disorder challenges or become dominated by dysfunction that drives away talented employees and undermines organizational effectiveness. Leaders need specific skills for managing complex interpersonal dynamics while maintaining team productivity and individual well-being.

Leadership competencies for psychologically safe environments include emotional regulation under pressure, fair treatment despite personal reactions, conflict resolution that addresses root causes, communication skills that de-escalate rather than inflame situations, and decision-making that balances individual needs with team effectiveness.

Training requirements go beyond general management development to include specific education about personality disorders, mental health awareness, legal compliance for accommodation and discrimination issues, and practical skills for managing challenging interpersonal situations. Leaders need both theoretical understanding and practical tools for real-world application.

Accountability systems ensure that leaders model appropriate behavior, address problems promptly, provide fair treatment to all employees, and create environments where psychological safety can flourish. Leadership accountability includes consequences for failing to address toxic behavior as well as recognition for creating positive workplace cultures.

Support structures provide leaders with resources they need to manage complex situations effectively, including HR consultation, legal guidance, mental health professional consultation, and peer support from other managers facing similar challenges. Leaders cannot create psychological safety without adequate support for their own professional development.

Performance measurement includes metrics that assess leaders' effectiveness at creating psychological safety, managing interpersonal challenges, and maintaining team productivity despite personality disorder impacts. These measurements help identify successful practices while providing feedback for continued improvement.

Sarah, a department director at a healthcare organization, exemplified effective leadership development when managing Robert, whose paranoid traits had created team tension and productivity challenges. Sarah participated in specialized training about mental health in the workplace, legal requirements for accommodation, and de-escalation techniques for managing suspicious or defensive behaviors. She developed skills for providing clear, documented communication that addressed Robert's concerns about hidden agendas while maintaining transparency with other team members. She learned to balance empathy for Robert's condition with accountability for professional behavior standards. When Robert's suspicions began affecting patient care coordination, Sarah addressed the situation promptly through structured conversations, clear documentation, and appropriate resource connections. Her leadership created psychological safety for other team members while providing Robert with support and clear expectations that helped him function more effectively.

Decision-making frameworks help leaders balance competing needs and interests when personality disorders affect team dynamics. These frameworks consider individual accommodation needs, team effectiveness requirements, organizational policy compliance, and legal obligations while providing clear processes for making difficult decisions.

Stress management for leaders becomes essential because managing personality disorder impacts creates additional stress that can affect judgment, emotional regulation, and decision-making quality. Leaders need personal strategies for maintaining their own well-being while supporting their teams effectively.

Continuous improvement involves regular assessment of leadership effectiveness, feedback from team members about psychological safety levels, and ongoing development of skills and knowledge that improve organizational culture and individual outcomes.

13.3 Policy Frameworks That Work

Effective policies provide clear guidance for creating and maintaining psychological safety while addressing personality disorder impacts fairly and legally. These policies must balance protection for individuals with mental health conditions against the need to maintain productive, safe workplace environments for all employees.

Behavioral standards define acceptable workplace conduct in specific terms that address common personality disorder manifestations without targeting mental health conditions directly. Standards might include requirements for respectful communication, collaborative decision-making, appropriate boundary maintenance, and professional conflict resolution.

Accommodation procedures outline how organizations will evaluate and implement reasonable accommodations for mental health conditions while maintaining essential job functions and workplace safety. These procedures must comply with legal requirements while providing practical guidance for managers and employees.

Complaint processes provide multiple avenues for addressing workplace concerns including informal resolution, formal grievance procedures, external reporting options, and anonymous feedback systems. Effective processes encourage early reporting while protecting complainants from retaliation.

Investigation protocols ensure fair, thorough evaluation of workplace concerns while protecting all parties' rights and maintaining confidentiality. Protocols must account for personality disorder impacts on perception and reporting while maintaining objectivity and legal compliance.

Consequences frameworks establish clear, consistent responses to policy violations while considering individual circumstances and accommodation needs. Frameworks must balance accountability with support while providing progressive intervention opportunities.

The technology consulting firm developed effective policy frameworks after experiencing several personality disorder-related workplace disruptions that had exposed gaps in their existing procedures. Their behavioral standards specified requirements for collaborative communication ("Team members will acknowledge others' contributions before presenting alternative viewpoints"), appropriate conflict resolution ("Disagreements will be addressed directly with involved parties rather than through complaints to uninvolved colleagues"), and professional boundary maintenance ("Personal information sharing will be limited to appropriate workplace relationships and contexts"). Their accommodation procedures provided clear steps for requesting and evaluating mental health accommodations while maintaining confidentiality and focusing on job-related impacts. Their complaint process included multiple reporting options, protection against retaliation, and timelines that prevented issues from escalating indefinitely. Most importantly, their consequence framework balanced accountability with support, providing intervention opportunities while maintaining clear standards for workplace behavior.

Policy communication ensures that all employees understand expectations, procedures, and available resources through training programs, written materials, supervisor discussions, and ongoing reinforcement. Effective communication prevents problems while building confidence that policies will be applied fairly.

Legal compliance requires regular review of policies to ensure alignment with changing employment laws, disability rights requirements, and court interpretations that affect workplace mental health accommodation. Legal review prevents discrimination while protecting organizational interests.

Cultural integration involves aligning policies with organizational values and practices in ways that support implementation and effectiveness. Policies that contradict organizational culture often fail in practice despite good intentions and legal compliance.

13.4 Measurement and Continuous Improvement

Measuring psychological safety and its impacts provides objective data for evaluating organizational effectiveness while identifying areas needing improvement or intervention. Effective measurement systems track both leading indicators that predict problems and lagging indicators that show results of organizational efforts.

Survey instruments assess employee perceptions of psychological safety, workplace culture, leadership effectiveness, and organizational support. Regular surveys provide trend data while anonymous formats encourage honest feedback about sensitive interpersonal issues.

Behavioral metrics track observable indicators of psychological safety including participation rates in meetings, frequency of innovation suggestions, error reporting rates, and conflict resolution effectiveness. These metrics provide objective data about actual workplace dynamics rather than just perceptions.

Performance indicators measure organizational outcomes that psychological safety influences including employee retention, productivity measures, customer satisfaction, and quality indicators. These broader metrics demonstrate the business value of psychological safety investments.

Incident tracking monitors workplace conflicts, harassment complaints, accommodation requests, and other indicators of interpersonal difficulty that might signal psychological safety problems. Trend analysis helps identify patterns while individual case review improves response effectiveness.

Cost analysis evaluates the financial impacts of psychological safety initiatives including reduced turnover, decreased conflicts, improved productivity, and lower legal risks. Cost data helps justify continued investment while identifying most effective interventions.

The financial services company implemented measurement systems after investing significantly in psychological safety improvements to address personality disorder impacts and wanted to evaluate their effectiveness. Their quarterly surveys measured employee perceptions of safety to speak up, leadership responsiveness, and team effectiveness. Their behavioral metrics tracked meeting participation rates, innovation suggestions submitted, and voluntary error reporting that indicated trust in organizational responses. Their performance indicators showed 30% reduction in turnover, 25% improvement in client satisfaction, and 40% decrease in HR complaints after implementing psychological safety initiatives. Their incident tracking revealed that conflicts were being reported and addressed earlier, preventing escalation to formal grievances or legal actions. Cost analysis showed that psychological safety investments had generated positive return on investment within 18 months through reduced recruiting costs, improved productivity, and decreased legal expenses.

Feedback loops ensure that measurement data influences organizational decision-making and improvement efforts rather than just providing interesting information. Regular review of metrics should drive specific actions that address identified problems and build on successful practices.

Benchmarking compares organizational performance to industry standards and best practices while identifying areas where improvement efforts might generate significant benefits. External benchmarks provide context for internal measurement while inspiring continued advancement.

Continuous improvement processes use measurement data to refine policies, training programs, leadership practices, and cultural initiatives that support psychological safety. Regular improvement cycles prevent stagnation while building organizational learning capabilities.

13.5 Technology Tools for Culture Management

Technology platforms provide powerful tools for creating, monitoring, and maintaining psychologically safe workplace cultures while addressing personality disorder impacts effectively. These tools can supplement traditional management approaches while providing data and capabilities that weren't previously available for culture management.

Communication platforms facilitate transparent, documented interactions that reduce misunderstandings while providing records that can address personality disorder-related disputes. Platforms that include features like meeting recording, collaborative document editing, and structured feedback systems help maintain professional communication standards.

Feedback systems enable anonymous reporting, continuous pulse surveys, and real-time culture monitoring that helps organizations identify problems early while tracking improvement efforts. Digital feedback tools often generate more honest responses than traditional methods while providing data analysis capabilities.

Training platforms deliver consistent education about psychological safety, personality disorder awareness, and workplace mental health through online modules, virtual reality simulations, and interactive scenarios. Technology-enabled training can provide personalized learning while ensuring consistent message delivery.

Analytics tools analyze communication patterns, collaboration effectiveness, and relationship networks to identify potential problems before they become serious workplace disruptions. Advanced analytics can detect changes in team dynamics that might indicate emerging personality disorder impacts.

Resource platforms connect employees with mental health resources, employee assistance programs, and support networks through confidential, accessible online portals. Technology platforms can reduce barriers to help-seeking while maintaining privacy and confidentiality.

The marketing agency implemented technology tools to support psychological safety after recognizing that personality disorder impacts were creating communication problems and team dysfunction that traditional management approaches hadn't addressed effectively. They adopted a communication platform that provided transparent project collaboration while maintaining records of decisions and feedback that prevented later disputes about what was said or agreed upon. Their feedback system enabled anonymous reporting of workplace concerns while providing managers with real-time culture data that helped them address problems early. Their analytics tools identified communication patterns that indicated team stress or relationship problems, allowing proactive intervention before conflicts escalated. Most importantly, their resource platform connected employees with mental health support while maintaining confidentiality and reducing stigma associated with help-seeking. These technology tools supplemented rather than replaced human management but provided capabilities that significantly improved their ability to maintain psychological safety despite interpersonal challenges.

Privacy protection ensures that technology tools maintain confidentiality while providing necessary information for organizational improvement. Balancing transparency with privacy requires careful design and implementation that protects individual rights while serving organizational needs.

Integration capabilities allow technology tools to work together effectively while avoiding duplicate data entry and conflicting information. Integrated systems provide comprehensive views of organizational culture while reducing administrative burden.

User adoption requires training, support, and incentives that encourage effective use of technology tools rather than resistance or superficial compliance. Successful adoption depends on demonstrating value while addressing concerns about privacy, complexity, or organizational change.

Return on investment measurement evaluates whether technology investments generate sufficient benefits to justify their costs while identifying most effective tools and implementation approaches. ROI analysis helps optimize technology spending while demonstrating value to organizational leadership.

Building Tomorrow's Foundation

Creating psychologically safe workplaces represents one of the most important investments organizations can make in their long-term success and sustainability. The effort required to build these environments pays dividends through improved innovation, stronger employee engagement, better customer relationships, and enhanced organizational resilience that serves companies well through changing business conditions.

The frameworks and tools presented here provide roadmaps for organizations at any stage of psychological safety development. Whether you're starting from scratch or refining existing efforts, these approaches offer practical strategies for creating workplace cultures where all employees can contribute their best work while maintaining their well-being and professional growth.

Psychological safety proves particularly important in environments where personality disorders create additional interpersonal challenges because it provides the foundation for addressing these challenges constructively rather than allowing them to undermine organizational effectiveness. When employees trust that problems will be addressed fairly and that they can speak up about concerns without retaliation, personality disorder impacts can be managed more effectively while protecting everyone's interests.

Most importantly, psychological safety initiatives often reveal organizational strengths and capabilities that extend far beyond managing individual personality challenges. The leadership skills, communication systems, and cultural practices that support psychological safety also improve overall organizational performance while creating environments where human potential can flourish.

The investment in building psychologically safe workplaces reflects organizational commitment to treating employees as whole human beings rather than just economic resources. This commitment often generates loyalty, creativity, and dedication that creates competitive advantages while building organizational cultures that attract and retain the best talent.

Core Safety Framework:

- The four pillars of psychological safety—predictable leadership, inclusive culture, learning orientation, and clear

accountability—provide foundation for environments where all employees can thrive
- Leadership development and accountability ensure that managers have skills and support necessary for creating and maintaining psychologically safe workplace cultures
- Policy frameworks balance protection for individuals with mental health conditions against organizational needs for productive, safe work environments
- Measurement and continuous improvement provide objective data for evaluating effectiveness while identifying areas needing attention or enhancement
- Technology tools supplement traditional management approaches while providing capabilities for monitoring, maintaining, and improving workplace cultures
- Psychological safety investments generate significant returns through improved performance, reduced conflicts, and enhanced organizational resilience

Chapter 14: Crisis Management and Professional Resources

The emergency room operates on the principle that early recognition and swift intervention can mean the difference between recovery and catastrophe. Staff members are trained to identify warning signs, follow established protocols, and know exactly when to call for specialized help that exceeds their own capabilities. Workplace mental health crises involving personality disorders require the same level of preparedness, clear protocols, and professional resource utilization to protect both individuals and organizations from potentially devastating outcomes.

Crisis situations don't announce themselves with advance warning—they develop from accumulating stress, escalating conflicts, or triggering events that overwhelm an individual's coping mechanisms. Organizations that prepare for these situations through crisis management planning, professional resource development, and staff training can respond effectively while minimizing harm to all involved parties.

14.1 Recognizing Mental Health Emergencies

Mental health emergencies in workplace settings involving personality disorders can escalate rapidly from interpersonal tension to situations that threaten safety, require immediate intervention, and exceed normal management capabilities. Recognition requires understanding the difference between typical personality disorder symptoms and crisis-level deterioration that demands immediate professional response.

Crisis indicators include threats of violence against self or others, complete break from reality that affects judgment and behavior, substance abuse that creates immediate safety concerns, severe emotional decompensation that prevents functioning, and behaviors that violate laws or create immediate liability risks for the organization.

Escalation patterns often follow predictable trajectories that provide warning opportunities for early intervention. These might include increasing frequency of emotional outbursts, progressive social isolation or paranoid thinking, growing instability in personal relationships, declining work performance despite increased effort, or mounting stress from multiple life areas that overwhelm coping abilities.

Suicidal ideation warning signs include verbal expressions of hopelessness, statements about wanting to die or disappear, giving away personal possessions, sudden mood improvement after severe depression, increased risk-taking behaviors, or preoccupation with death and dying. These signs require immediate attention regardless of personality disorder diagnosis.

Violence risk indicators encompass threats against specific individuals, fascination with weapons or violent events, history of aggressive behavior that's escalating, paranoid beliefs about persecution or threats, or statements about "teaching lessons" to people who have "wronged" them. Violence risk assessment requires professional expertise and immediate intervention.

Psychotic symptoms may include hearing voices, seeing things others don't see, believing things that clearly aren't true, speaking incoherently, or showing severe confusion about time, place, or identity. Psychotic symptoms can occur during severe personality disorder episodes and require immediate medical attention.

Margaret, an HR director at a manufacturing company, recognized crisis indicators when David, whose antisocial traits had created ongoing workplace problems, began showing escalating concerning behaviors. His usual manipulation and rule-breaking had progressed to making veiled threats against colleagues who had reported his misconduct ("people who can't mind their own business sometimes learn hard lessons"), expressing paranoid beliefs about "conspiracies" to get him fired, and showing up to work under the influence of alcohol. When a female colleague reported that David had followed her to her car and made threatening comments about "teaching her to respect men," Margaret recognized these as crisis-level indicators requiring immediate intervention. She contacted the employee assistance program crisis line, consulted with legal counsel about safety measures, and implemented emergency procedures to protect the threatened employee while addressing David's deteriorating condition.

Substance abuse complications can rapidly escalate personality disorder symptoms into crisis situations. Alcohol or drug use often removes whatever inhibitions or coping mechanisms help individuals manage their personality disorder symptoms, leading to impulsive, aggressive, or dangerous behaviors that create immediate risks.

Environmental triggers that can precipitate crises include major life stressors like divorce or financial problems, workplace changes such as reorganizations or new supervisors, anniversary dates of traumatic events, or seasonal factors that affect mood and behavior. Understanding these triggers helps predict and prevent crisis situations when possible.

Response protocols must distinguish between situations requiring immediate emergency intervention (calling 911, involving law enforcement, or emergency medical services) versus those needing urgent but less immediate professional response (employee assistance programs, mental health crisis teams, or organizational crisis management procedures).

Documentation requirements for crisis situations include specific behavioral observations, exact quotes when possible, witness information, timeline of events, and immediate safety measures taken. This documentation supports appropriate intervention while protecting legal interests and providing information for professional responders.

14.2 EAP Integration and Utilization

Employee Assistance Programs provide front-line resources for addressing mental health crises while connecting individuals with professional services that exceed organizational capabilities. Effective EAP integration requires understanding program capabilities, limitations, and appropriate utilization procedures that serve both individual and organizational needs.

EAP services typically include crisis intervention support, short-term counseling, referrals to community mental health resources, workplace consultation for managers, and emergency response assistance during mental health crises. Understanding these services helps organizations utilize EAPs effectively while maintaining appropriate boundaries.

Crisis intervention capabilities allow EAPs to provide immediate support during mental health emergencies through 24-hour hotlines, emergency counseling services, safety planning assistance, and coordination with other professional resources. Most EAPs can respond to crisis situations much faster than traditional mental health services.

Management consultation helps supervisors and HR personnel navigate complex situations involving mental health concerns through confidential guidance about response options, legal requirements, accommodation possibilities, and resource recommendations. This consultation protects both individual and organizational interests.

Referral coordination connects individuals with appropriate long-term mental health services, substance abuse treatment, legal assistance, or other community resources that address underlying issues contributing to workplace problems. EAPs often have better knowledge of available resources than organizational staff.

Follow-up services provide ongoing support and monitoring to ensure that crisis interventions are effective and that individuals receive continued assistance needed for stability and recovery.

Follow-up prevents crisis recurrence while supporting successful workplace integration.

Jennifer, a department manager at a technology company, effectively utilized EAP services when Lisa, whose borderline traits had created ongoing team disruption, experienced a mental health crisis following a relationship breakup that affected her workplace behavior dramatically. Lisa began having emotional outbursts that lasted hours, making statements about not wanting to live anymore, and engaging in self-harm behaviors that colleagues witnessed. Jennifer immediately contacted the EAP crisis line, which provided immediate phone support for Lisa while guiding Jennifer through safety protocols and documentation requirements. The EAP counselor conducted a suicide risk assessment, developed a safety plan with Lisa, and arranged for immediate mental health evaluation. They also provided Jennifer with guidance about workplace accommodations that might support Lisa's recovery while maintaining team productivity. The EAP continued follow-up services for several weeks, helping Lisa access ongoing mental health treatment while supporting her gradual return to normal workplace functioning.

Confidentiality protections ensure that EAP services maintain privacy while providing necessary information for workplace safety and accommodation. Understanding confidentiality boundaries helps managers utilize EAP resources appropriately while protecting individual rights.

Legal compliance requires understanding how EAP utilization relates to accommodation obligations, documentation requirements, and privacy protections under various employment laws. EAP staff can provide guidance about legal compliance while maintaining focus on individual well-being.

Cost considerations involve understanding what EAP services are covered under organizational contracts versus individual responsibility for ongoing treatment costs. Clear understanding prevents surprises while ensuring appropriate resource utilization.

Quality assessment evaluates EAP effectiveness through outcome measures, user satisfaction, and organizational impact indicators. Regular assessment helps optimize EAP utilization while identifying needs for additional resources or service modifications.

14.3 When to Involve Legal Counsel

Legal consultation becomes necessary when personality disorder situations create potential liability risks, violate employment laws, or require specialized expertise that exceeds organizational capabilities. Understanding when to seek legal advice protects both individual and organizational interests while ensuring appropriate response to complex situations.

Legal consultation triggers include threats of violence or harassment, discrimination or accommodation complaints, potential wrongful termination situations, safety concerns that might require restrictive actions, whistleblower or retaliation claims, and any situation involving law enforcement or criminal behavior.

Employment law expertise provides guidance about accommodation requirements, progressive discipline procedures, termination considerations, and documentation standards that protect against discrimination claims while maintaining workplace safety and productivity.

Risk assessment helps organizations evaluate potential legal exposure from personality disorder situations while developing strategies that minimize liability while addressing legitimate business concerns and employee welfare.

Documentation review ensures that organizational records support appropriate personnel decisions while meeting legal standards for objective evaluation and fair treatment. Legal review can identify gaps or problems in documentation before they become litigation issues.

Policy compliance verification confirms that organizational responses follow established procedures and legal requirements while identifying areas where policy modification might reduce future risks or improve effectiveness.

Michael, a human resources director at a financial services company, sought legal consultation when Robert, whose paranoid traits had created ongoing workplace tensions, filed discrimination complaints claiming persecution and harassment by supervisors and colleagues. Robert alleged that normal performance management discussions were actually discrimination against his mental health condition, that colleagues' avoidance of his suspicious and accusatory behavior constituted harassment, and that the organization was creating a hostile work environment. Legal counsel reviewed all documentation, interviewed relevant witnesses, and assessed the organization's accommodation efforts and policy compliance. They determined that the organization had followed appropriate procedures and provided reasonable accommodations, but recommended enhanced documentation practices and modified communication protocols to prevent future complaints. Legal guidance helped the organization respond appropriately to regulatory investigations while maintaining necessary performance standards and workplace safety.

Accommodation analysis determines what workplace modifications might be legally required while distinguishing between reasonable accommodations and undue hardship that organizations aren't obligated to provide. Legal expertise prevents both inadequate accommodation and excessive burden.

Termination planning involves legal review of documentation, procedures, and timing to minimize wrongful discharge risks while protecting organizational interests. Legal counsel can identify potential problems and recommend strategies that support defensible employment decisions.

Crisis response may require immediate legal consultation when personality disorder situations involve criminal behavior, safety threats, or regulatory reporting requirements. Emergency legal consultation helps organizations respond appropriately while protecting all parties' interests.

Litigation management provides representation and guidance when personality disorder situations result in formal legal proceedings, regulatory investigations, or administrative complaints. Experienced employment counsel can navigate these complex situations while minimizing organizational disruption.

14.4 Fitness for Duty Evaluations

Fitness for duty evaluations provide objective professional assessment of employees' ability to perform essential job functions safely and effectively when mental health concerns affect workplace performance. These evaluations help organizations make informed decisions about accommodation, modification, or restriction of work duties while protecting individual rights and organizational interests.

Evaluation triggers include safety incidents that might relate to mental health conditions, significant performance deterioration despite normal interventions, behaviors that create concerns about judgment or decision-making capacity, accommodation requests that require understanding of functional limitations, or situations where fitness questions arise from observed behavioral changes.

Professional qualifications for fitness evaluations require licensed mental health professionals with expertise in occupational assessment, personality disorders, and workplace functioning. Evaluators must understand both clinical assessment and job requirements to provide meaningful recommendations.

Evaluation components typically include clinical interviews, psychological testing, review of medical and employment records, assessment of job-related functional capabilities, and specific recommendations about workplace modifications or restrictions that might support successful functioning.

Legal requirements govern how fitness evaluations are requested, conducted, and utilized in employment decisions. These requirements protect employee privacy while ensuring that evaluations are job-related and consistent with business necessity.

Accommodation recommendations from fitness evaluations help organizations understand what workplace modifications might enable successful job performance while identifying limitations that might require alternative assignments or accommodations.

Sarah, a department supervisor at a healthcare organization, requested fitness for duty evaluation when Patricia, whose histrionic traits had been manageable with accommodations, began showing deteriorating judgment and emotional regulation that affected patient care. Patricia had started sharing inappropriate personal information with patients, becoming emotionally distraught during routine care situations, and making clinical decisions based on emotional reactions rather than professional protocols. The fitness evaluation included comprehensive clinical assessment, review of Patricia's employment history and accommodation records, psychological testing to assess functional capabilities, and specific evaluation of her ability to maintain professional boundaries and clinical judgment under stress. The evaluator recommended continued employment with modified assignments that reduced direct patient contact while Patricia received intensive mental health treatment, along with enhanced supervision and structured support during her recovery process.

Evaluation process must be conducted fairly and consistently while maintaining confidentiality and focusing on job-related functional assessment. Proper process protects both individual rights and organizational interests while providing objective information for decision-making.

Result interpretation requires understanding how clinical findings relate to specific job requirements and what accommodations might address identified limitations. Professional interpretation helps translate clinical information into practical workplace recommendations.

Implementation planning uses evaluation recommendations to develop specific accommodation plans, workplace modifications, or alternative assignments that support individual success while maintaining organizational effectiveness and safety standards.

Follow-up procedures monitor implementation effectiveness while providing ongoing assessment of functional improvement or deterioration that might require modification of workplace accommodations or assignments.

14.5 Return-to-Work Planning

Return-to-work planning helps employees transition successfully back to workplace responsibilities after mental health crises, treatment periods, or extended absences while ensuring that underlying issues have been adequately addressed to prevent recurrence of problems.

Assessment requirements determine readiness for work return through medical clearance, functional capacity evaluation, and assessment of trigger management and coping skill development. Comprehensive assessment prevents premature return that might lead to crisis recurrence.

Accommodation planning modifies workplace conditions, assignments, or schedules to support successful reintegration while addressing ongoing mental health needs. Accommodations should be based on current functional assessment rather than assumptions about previous capabilities.

Gradual reintegration allows step-by-step return to full responsibilities through reduced hours, modified assignments, or enhanced supervision that supports adjustment while monitoring stability. Gradual approaches often prove more successful than immediate full return.

Support system activation connects returning employees with ongoing resources including employee assistance programs, mental health treatment, peer support, and supervisory assistance that maintain stability and prevent crisis recurrence.

Monitoring protocols track adjustment success through regular check-ins, performance assessment, and ongoing evaluation of accommodation effectiveness. Monitoring allows early intervention if problems emerge while supporting continued success.

David, an operations manager, developed return-to-work planning for Marcus, whose narcissistic traits had escalated into a mental health crisis involving severe depression and anxiety that required hospitalization and intensive treatment. Marcus's return planning included medical clearance confirming his stability and readiness for work stress, functional assessment showing his ability to handle collaborative work and feedback appropriately, and accommodation plan that included modified project assignments reducing high-visibility presentations that had previously triggered grandiose behaviors. His gradual reintegration started with part-time hours and individual projects, progressing to full-time collaborative work over six weeks. Support systems included weekly EAP check-ins, monthly supervisory meetings focused on accommodation effectiveness, and continued mental health treatment that addressed underlying issues. Monitoring protocols included performance metrics, team feedback, and early warning indicators of stress or symptom recurrence that might require additional intervention.

Legal compliance ensures return-to-work planning meets accommodation requirements while maintaining essential job functions and workplace safety. Legal compliance protects both individual rights and organizational interests throughout the return process.

Team preparation helps colleagues understand appropriate responses to returning employees while maintaining confidentiality and supporting successful reintegration. Team preparation prevents awkwardness while building supportive relationships.

Success indicators measure return-to-work effectiveness through performance metrics, stability indicators, and accommodation success measures. Clear indicators help evaluate program effectiveness while identifying areas for improvement.

Contingency planning prepares for potential setbacks or crisis recurrence through early warning systems, rapid response procedures, and alternative accommodation options. Contingency planning supports long-term success while protecting all parties if problems recur.

Wisdom from the Front Lines

Crisis management in workplace settings reminds us that behind every personality disorder diagnosis lies a human being who is struggling with conditions they didn't choose and may not fully understand. The professional resources and intervention strategies presented here serve both compassionate and practical purposes—they protect organizational interests while providing pathways to recovery and stability that benefit everyone involved.

The most effective organizations recognize that mental health crises are medical emergencies that require professional response rather than amateur intervention or wishful thinking that problems will resolve themselves. They invest in crisis management capabilities, develop relationships with professional resources, and train their staff to recognize when situations exceed normal management capabilities.

However, crisis management alone isn't sufficient—it must be combined with prevention efforts, early intervention systems, and ongoing support that address underlying issues before they reach crisis levels. The goal isn't to become expert in managing mental health emergencies but to create workplace environments where such emergencies are rare and, when they do occur, are handled with skill and compassion.

Professional resources exist to support both individuals and organizations through these challenging situations. Utilizing these resources effectively requires understanding their capabilities, limitations, and appropriate applications while maintaining realistic expectations about what can be achieved through workplace interventions versus clinical treatment.

Most importantly, crisis management capabilities demonstrate organizational commitment to treating employees as whole human beings deserving of care and support during their most difficult moments. This commitment often generates loyalty and dedication that extends far beyond immediate crisis situations while building organizational cultures that attract and retain employees who value working for employers who care about their well-being.

Essential Crisis Response Framework:

- Mental health emergency recognition requires understanding crisis indicators that distinguish between typical personality disorder symptoms and situations requiring immediate professional intervention
- EAP integration provides front-line crisis support while connecting individuals with professional services that exceed organizational capabilities
- Legal counsel becomes necessary when personality disorder situations create liability risks or require specialized expertise beyond normal HR capabilities
- Fitness for duty evaluations provide objective assessment of workplace functioning while supporting appropriate accommodation and return-to-work planning
- Return-to-work planning ensures successful reintegration after mental health crises while preventing recurrence through ongoing support and monitoring
- Crisis management demonstrates organizational commitment to employee well-being while protecting all parties through professional resource utilization

Chapter 15: Emerging Trends and Future Workplace Evolution

The meteorologist who studies only yesterday's weather patterns will miss the gathering storm clouds that shape tomorrow's forecast. Similarly, understanding personality disorders in workplace settings requires looking beyond current challenges to recognize emerging trends that will reshape how we work, communicate, and support each other in an increasingly complex professional world.

The rapid acceleration of remote work, artificial intelligence integration, generational shifts in mental health awareness, and post-pandemic workplace transformations are creating new contexts for personality disorder manifestations while offering unprecedented opportunities for support, accommodation, and early intervention. Organizations that prepare for these emerging realities will be better positioned to create healthy, productive workplace cultures that serve all employees effectively.

15.1 Remote Work and Virtual Toxicity

Remote work environments fundamentally alter how personality disorders manifest and affect workplace relationships while creating new challenges for recognition, intervention, and management that traditional in-person strategies may not address effectively. Virtual interactions can both mask and amplify personality disorder symptoms depending on the specific condition and individual coping mechanisms.

Digital communication impacts change how personality disorders affect workplace relationships because virtual interactions filter out many social cues, reduce spontaneous relationship building, and create permanent records of communications that can be analyzed or misinterpreted later. Email and video calls may reduce the immediate emotional impact of some personality disorders while amplifying others that thrive on digital manipulation.

Isolation effects can worsen certain personality disorder symptoms by reducing social feedback, eliminating casual relationship building, and creating conditions where problematic thinking patterns can develop without reality-checking from colleagues. Individuals with paranoid traits may become more suspicious, those with borderline patterns may feel more abandoned, and narcissistic individuals may lose opportunities for attention and admiration.

Control and manipulation adaptations show how personality-disordered individuals modify their behaviors for virtual environments. Some may use technology to increase monitoring and control of colleagues, others might manipulate meeting participation to dominate discussions, and some could exploit remote work flexibility to avoid accountability or responsibilities.

Virtual boundary violations create new categories of inappropriate workplace behavior including excessive personal sharing during video calls, inappropriate digital communications, invasion of colleagues' personal spaces through technology, and manipulation of virtual meeting dynamics to create drama or attention.

Marcus, whose narcissistic traits had previously disrupted in-person team meetings, adapted his behavior patterns to remote work by dominating video calls through constant screen sharing of his work, sending lengthy emails that copied multiple people unnecessarily to showcase his involvement, and scheduling individual meetings with senior leaders to position himself as indispensable. His virtual behavior created different but equally disruptive team dynamics as colleagues felt unable to contribute meaningfully during his presentations and became exhausted by his excessive digital communications. Team productivity declined as meetings became platforms for Marcus's self-promotion rather than collaborative problem-solving sessions.

Recognition challenges in remote environments include reduced visibility of behavioral patterns, difficulty distinguishing between technical problems and interpersonal issues, limited ability to observe non-verbal cues that indicate emotional states, and challenges in building trust relationships that support intervention and accommodation efforts.

Intervention modifications for remote environments require different approaches than in-person strategies. These might include structured video meeting protocols that prevent domination, digital documentation systems that track behavioral patterns, virtual coaching and support resources, and modified supervision approaches that account for reduced direct observation.

Technology exploitation shows how personality-disordered individuals may use digital tools manipulatively, such as selective screen sharing to control information, strategic use of private messaging to create alliances or spread rumors, manipulation of meeting recording features, or exploitation of flexible schedules to avoid accountability.

Virtual team resilience requires intentional development of online relationship building, digital communication norms, remote conflict resolution processes, and technology-mediated support systems that protect team members from virtual toxicity while maintaining productivity and collaboration.

15.2 AI and Technology in Behavior Management

Artificial intelligence and advanced technology platforms are creating unprecedented opportunities for early detection, intervention, and management of personality disorder impacts in workplace settings while raising important questions about privacy, autonomy, and the role of technology in human relationship management.

Pattern recognition systems can analyze communication patterns, collaboration metrics, and behavioral indicators to identify potential personality disorder impacts before they become obvious to human observers. Machine learning algorithms can detect subtle changes in email tone, meeting participation, or work quality that might indicate emerging problems.

Predictive analytics use historical data and behavioral patterns to forecast potential workplace conflicts, identify individuals at risk for crisis situations, and recommend intervention timing that maximizes effectiveness while minimizing disruption. Predictive systems can suggest optimal approaches for managing specific personality types based on successful interventions with similar individuals.

Automated intervention triggers can initiate support resources, coaching opportunities, or managerial attention when behavioral patterns indicate emerging problems. These systems can provide early warning alerts while maintaining privacy and reducing stigma associated with mental health concerns.

Communication analysis tools can evaluate email tone, meeting dynamics, and collaborative interactions to identify concerning patterns while providing feedback that helps individuals modify their communication approaches. Real-time analysis can prevent problematic interactions while supporting skill development.

Personalized accommodation recommendations use individual behavioral data and job requirements to suggest specific workplace modifications that might improve functioning while maintaining productivity. AI systems can identify accommodation patterns that have been successful for similar situations while considering legal and practical constraints.

The consulting firm implemented AI-powered behavior management tools after recognizing that personality disorder impacts were creating patterns they couldn't detect early enough for effective intervention. Their communication analysis system identified concerning changes in Jennifer's email patterns that indicated increasing emotional volatility before colleagues noticed behavioral changes. The system flagged messages with increasingly negative sentiment, excessive emotional language, and departure from her normal communication style. These early indicators allowed her supervisor to provide proactive support and accommodation adjustments that prevented a crisis situation. The AI system also identified successful intervention patterns from previous cases that guided their response strategy. Over time, the system learned to recognize her specific stress indicators and provided increasingly accurate recommendations for timing and type of support interventions.

Privacy considerations require balancing behavior monitoring capabilities with employee rights to privacy and autonomy. Organizations must establish clear policies about what data is collected, how it's analyzed, and who has access to behavioral insights while maintaining legal compliance and ethical standards.

Bias prevention ensures that AI systems don't perpetuate discrimination against individuals with mental health conditions or personality disorders. Algorithm development must include bias testing, diverse training data, and ongoing monitoring to prevent unfair treatment based on protected characteristics.

Human oversight maintains final decision-making authority with qualified professionals while using AI insights to inform but not replace human judgment about accommodation, intervention, and management decisions. Technology should augment rather than replace human expertise in complex interpersonal situations.

Effectiveness measurement tracks whether AI-enabled behavior management actually improves outcomes compared to traditional approaches while identifying unintended consequences or limitations that require system modifications.

15.3 Generational Differences in Mental Health Approaches

Generational shifts in mental health awareness, stigma reduction, and help-seeking behaviors are creating new opportunities and challenges for managing personality disorders in workplace settings as different age groups bring varying expectations and approaches to mental health issues.

Stigma reduction trends among younger generations create environments where mental health discussions are more open and accepted, potentially leading to earlier identification and intervention for personality disorder issues. However, increased openness may also create expectations for accommodation that exceed legal requirements or organizational capabilities.

Help-seeking behaviors vary significantly across generations, with younger employees more likely to seek mental health support early while older employees may view such help-seeking as weakness or professional liability. These differences affect how personality disorder impacts are recognized and addressed across different age groups.

Communication preferences about mental health vary by generation, with younger employees often preferring digital platforms and peer support networks while older employees may prefer traditional hierarchical support through supervisors or formal employee assistance programs.

Accommodation expectations differ across generations, with younger employees often expecting immediate and comprehensive workplace modifications while older employees may be more resistant to accommodations that they perceive as special treatment or professional weakness.

Disclosure patterns show generational differences in willingness to share mental health information with employers, colleagues, and supervisors. Understanding these patterns helps organizations develop age-appropriate support strategies while respecting individual preferences.

The marketing department experienced generational differences when managing personality disorder impacts across their age-diverse team. Sarah, a 24-year-old analyst with borderline traits, was open about her mental health challenges and actively sought workplace accommodations including flexible scheduling, private workspace, and modified feedback approaches. She used the company's mental health benefits extensively and participated in peer support groups. In contrast, Robert, a 58-year-old director with obsessive-compulsive traits, was resistant to any discussion of mental health accommodations despite obvious impacts on team productivity. He viewed accommodation suggestions as questioning his competence and preferred to manage his perfectionist tendencies through increased work hours and detailed planning. The department had to develop different support approaches for each individual while maintaining fairness and legal compliance across generational differences.

Training modifications must account for generational learning preferences and comfort levels with mental health topics. Younger employees may prefer interactive, digital training platforms while older employees might respond better to traditional classroom or one-on-one educational approaches.

Support system design should offer multiple options that appeal to different generational preferences including peer networks, digital resources, traditional employee assistance programs, and hierarchical support structures. Diverse options ensure that all age groups can access help effectively.

Communication strategies must adapt to generational preferences while maintaining consistent organizational messages about mental health support and accommodation. This might include multiple communication channels, varied messaging styles, and age-appropriate resource recommendations.

Leadership development needs to prepare managers for supervising employees from different generations with varying mental health awareness and expectations. Leaders must understand generational differences while maintaining consistent standards and fair treatment.

15.4 The Post-Pandemic Workplace Mental Health Revolution

The COVID-19 pandemic accelerated mental health awareness and accommodation practices while creating new stress factors that may trigger or worsen personality disorder symptoms. Understanding these post-pandemic changes helps organizations adapt their approaches to meet emerging needs while building on increased mental health acceptance.

Increased mental health awareness has reduced stigma and created greater organizational willingness to address mental health issues proactively. This awareness creates opportunities for earlier intervention and better support for personality disorder impacts while also raising expectations for organizational response.

Stress amplification effects from pandemic-related changes may have worsened existing personality disorder symptoms or triggered new episodes among individuals who were previously stable. Organizations must be prepared for increased mental health needs while maintaining appropriate boundaries and support.

Flexibility expectations have increased dramatically as employees experienced remote work and alternative scheduling options during pandemic restrictions. These expectations create opportunities for accommodation while also challenging traditional work structures and management approaches.

Social connection challenges from extended isolation and remote work may have particularly affected individuals with personality disorders who struggle with relationship building and maintenance. Organizations need strategies for rebuilding social connections while preventing toxic relationship patterns.

Economic stress impacts from pandemic-related financial insecurity may have triggered or worsened personality disorder symptoms, particularly among individuals with traits involving emotional volatility, paranoid thinking, or difficulty managing stress and uncertainty.

The technology company experienced significant post-pandemic mental health challenges when David, whose antisocial traits had been manageable before COVID-19, showed deteriorating behavior patterns after experiencing job insecurity and social isolation during lockdowns. His manipulation and exploitation of colleagues became more pronounced as he struggled with financial stress and reduced social connections. However, the company's increased mental health awareness and expanded employee assistance programs provided better resources for addressing his behavior impacts while supporting affected colleagues. The organization had learned to recognize personality disorder symptoms earlier and respond more effectively through improved training and support systems developed during the pandemic.

Accommodation evolution shows how pandemic experiences expanded organizational understanding of what workplace modifications are possible while maintaining productivity. This evolution creates new opportunities for supporting individuals with personality disorders through flexible arrangements that weren't previously considered.

Mental health integration involves incorporating mental health considerations into all aspects of workplace planning and management rather than treating them as separate issues. This integration improves support for personality disorder impacts while reducing stigma and increasing early intervention.

Crisis response improvement builds on pandemic experiences with emergency planning and rapid adaptation to create better systems for managing mental health crises and supporting employees through difficult periods.

Recovery planning helps organizations and individuals develop resilience and coping strategies that prevent or minimize personality disorder impacts during future disruptions or challenging periods.

15.5 Building Antifragile Organizations

Antifragile organizations don't just survive challenges—they actually become stronger through adversity by developing capabilities that serve them well beyond the specific difficulties they originally faced. Building antifragile responses to personality disorder challenges creates organizational strengths that improve overall effectiveness while preparing for future uncertainties.

Adaptive capacity involves developing organizational flexibility that allows rapid response to changing conditions while maintaining core values and functions. This capacity helps organizations adjust their approaches to personality disorder management as new challenges and opportunities emerge.

Learning integration builds systems that capture knowledge from managing personality disorder challenges and apply these lessons to improve overall organizational effectiveness. Learning organizations convert difficult experiences into capabilities that strengthen future performance.

Resilience multiplication creates strength that extends beyond specific individuals or situations to improve organizational capacity for handling various types of challenges. Skills developed managing personality disorders often apply to other interpersonal and leadership challenges.

Innovation acceleration uses challenges as opportunities to develop new approaches, technologies, and capabilities that provide competitive advantages while solving immediate problems. Organizations that innovate in response to personality disorder challenges often discover broader applications for their solutions.

Culture strengthening involves using difficult situations to clarify values, improve communication, and build stronger relationships among team members who work together effectively to address challenges. Shared adversity often strengthens organizational culture when handled well.

The healthcare organization became antifragile through their experience managing multiple personality disorder challenges by developing sophisticated interpersonal skills, conflict resolution capabilities, and support systems that improved their overall organizational effectiveness. Their investment in training managers to handle complex behavioral situations created leadership capabilities that served them well in various challenging circumstances. Their development of employee support systems and crisis management protocols provided frameworks that helped them navigate other types of organizational difficulties. Most importantly, their experience building psychologically safe environments while managing personality disorder impacts created organizational culture that attracted high-quality employees and supported innovation and excellence across all areas of operation.

Continuous improvement systems ensure that lessons learned from personality disorder management are captured and applied to ongoing organizational development rather than being lost when specific individuals or situations change.

Knowledge management preserves and shares expertise about managing personality disorder impacts while building organizational memory that supports consistent and effective responses over time.

Capability building uses personality disorder challenges as opportunities to develop skills, systems, and resources that strengthen overall organizational effectiveness while serving immediate needs.

Future preparation involves using current experiences to anticipate and prepare for future challenges while building flexibility and resilience that serve organizations well regardless of specific difficulties they may face.

Glimpsing Tomorrow's Possibilities

The future of personality disorders in workplace settings will be shaped by technological advances, generational changes, and evolving understanding of mental health that create both new challenges and unprecedented opportunities for support, accommodation, and early intervention. Organizations that prepare for these emerging realities will be better positioned to create healthy, productive workplace cultures that serve all employees effectively.

The trends discussed here suggest that mental health awareness will continue increasing while technology provides new tools for recognition and intervention. Generational differences will require adaptable approaches that meet varying needs and expectations while maintaining consistent organizational standards and values.

Most importantly, the post-pandemic acceleration of mental health awareness has created opportunities for organizations to build antifragile capabilities that serve them well beyond specific personality disorder challenges. The skills, systems, and cultural practices developed for managing these complex interpersonal situations often strengthen overall organizational effectiveness while preparing for various types of future challenges.

The key to success lies in viewing personality disorder challenges as opportunities for growth and learning rather than problems to be endured. Organizations that embrace this perspective often discover that their investment in building sophisticated interpersonal capabilities creates competitive advantages while fulfilling their obligations to treat all employees with dignity and respect.

As we look toward the future, the goal isn't to predict every change that will affect workplace personality dynamics but to build organizational capabilities that remain effective regardless of specific challenges. The principles of psychological safety, early intervention, professional resource utilization, and continuous learning provide foundations that serve organizations well through changing conditions while supporting human flourishing in all its complexity.

Future-Ready Strategies:

- Remote work environments require new approaches to recognition and intervention that account for virtual interaction challenges while leveraging technology capabilities
- AI and advanced analytics provide unprecedented opportunities for early detection and personalized intervention while requiring careful attention to privacy and bias prevention

- Generational differences in mental health approaches require adaptable support systems that meet varying needs while maintaining consistent organizational standards
- Post-pandemic mental health awareness creates opportunities for improved accommodation and support while raising expectations for organizational responsiveness
- Antifragile organizations use personality disorder challenges as opportunities to build capabilities that strengthen overall effectiveness and prepare for future uncertainties
- Success requires viewing personality disorder challenges as learning opportunities rather than problems to be endured

Appendix A: Quick Reference Guides

Personality Disorder Characteristics Cheat Sheet

This essential reference provides immediate access to key diagnostic criteria and workplace manifestations for each personality disorder type, enabling quick identification and appropriate response strategies.

Cluster A (Odd/Eccentric) Disorders:

Paranoid Personality Disorder

- Core features: Pervasive distrust and suspiciousness of others
- Workplace signs: Questions colleagues' motives, reluctant to share information, interprets benign comments as attacks, holds grudges over minor incidents
- Management approach: Provide written documentation, maintain transparency, avoid taking suspicions personally, offer clear explanations for decisions

Schizoid Personality Disorder

- Core features: Detachment from social relationships, restricted emotional expression
- Workplace signs: Prefers solitary work, shows little interest in team activities, appears emotionally cold, indifferent to praise or criticism
- Management approach: Respect need for independence, don't force social interaction, focus on work quality rather than team integration

Schizotypal Personality Disorder

- Core features: Acute discomfort in relationships, cognitive distortions, eccentric behavior

- Workplace signs: Odd beliefs about workplace events, unusual perceptual experiences, peculiar speech patterns, eccentric appearance
- Management approach: Maintain professional boundaries, avoid reinforcing unusual beliefs, provide clear structure and expectations

Cluster B (Dramatic/Emotional/Erratic) Disorders:

Narcissistic Personality Disorder

- Core features: Grandiose self-perception, need for admiration, lack of empathy
- Workplace signs: Takes credit for others' work, expects special treatment, shows no empathy for colleagues' needs, becomes enraged when criticized
- Management approach: Acknowledge competence while addressing behavior, provide feedback that preserves self-esteem, set clear boundaries about team collaboration

Borderline Personality Disorder

- Core features: Instability in relationships, self-image, emotions, and marked impulsivity
- Workplace signs: Intense unstable relationships, emotional volatility, frantic efforts to avoid abandonment, identity disturbance
- Management approach: Provide consistent support, use clear written communication, offer emotional regulation breaks, maintain relationship stability

Antisocial Personality Disorder

- Core features: Disregard for and violation of others' rights
- Workplace signs: Deceitfulness, manipulation, disregard for safety, lack of remorse for harmful actions, consistent irresponsibility

- Management approach: Focus on consequences rather than empathy, document everything, maintain clear policies, monitor compliance closely

Histrionic Personality Disorder

- Core features: Excessive emotionality and attention-seeking
- Workplace signs: Uncomfortable when not center of attention, inappropriate emotional expression, considers relationships more intimate than they are
- Management approach: Provide structured attention, redirect dramatic behavior, maintain professional boundaries, acknowledge contributions appropriately

Cluster C (Anxious/Fearful) Disorders:

Avoidant Personality Disorder

- Core features: Social inhibition, feelings of inadequacy, hypersensitivity to criticism
- Workplace signs: Avoids interpersonal contact, reluctant to take risks, preoccupied with criticism, inhibited in new situations
- Management approach: Provide encouragement and support, offer gradual exposure to challenging situations, give positive feedback frequently

Dependent Personality Disorder

- Core features: Excessive need for care, submissive behavior, fears of separation
- Workplace signs: Difficulty making decisions without excessive advice, needs others to assume responsibility, difficulty expressing disagreement
- Management approach: Encourage independent decision-making, provide structured support, gradually increase responsibility

Obsessive-Compulsive Personality Disorder

- Core features: Preoccupation with orderliness, perfectionism, and control
- Workplace signs: Perfectionism interferes with completion, excessive devotion to work, inflexible about procedures, reluctant to delegate
- Management approach: Set realistic deadlines, help prioritize tasks, encourage delegation, balance quality with efficiency

Communication Strategies by Type

For Narcissistic Individuals:

- Begin with acknowledgment of their competence or contributions
- Frame feedback as opportunities to enhance already strong performance
- Use collaborative language that positions you as supporting their success
- Avoid global statements about personality; focus on specific behaviors
- Provide written follow-up to verbal discussions

For Borderline Individuals:

- Start conversations with explicit relationship reassurance
- Break complex feedback into smaller, manageable pieces
- Provide specific examples rather than general observations
- End with clear next steps and follow-up commitments
- Be prepared for emotional reactions and have support resources available

For Antisocial Individuals:

- Focus on specific behaviors and their direct consequences
- Provide clear expectations with explicit outcomes
- Document everything and follow through consistently

- Avoid emotional appeals; use logical cause-and-effect reasoning
- Maintain professional boundaries and don't take manipulation personally

For Paranoid Individuals:

- Provide extra explanations for decisions and policies
- Use written communication to prevent misinterpretation
- Be transparent about intentions and processes
- Avoid taking suspicions personally or becoming defensive
- Offer documentation to support explanations

Legal Compliance Checklist

Pre-Employment Screening:

- ☐ Questions focus on job-related behaviors and skills
- ☐ No direct inquiries about mental health history or diagnoses
- ☐ Consistent evaluation criteria applied to all candidates
- ☐ Documentation supports hiring decisions with objective criteria
- ☐ Reference checks focus on work performance and observable behaviors

Accommodation Process:

- ☐ Interactive process initiated when accommodation need identified
- ☐ Medical documentation obtained from qualified professionals
- ☐ Essential job functions identified and analyzed
- ☐ Reasonable accommodations explored and documented
- ☐ Undue hardship analysis conducted when applicable
- ☐ Regular review of accommodation effectiveness scheduled

Performance Management:

- ☐ Clear behavioral expectations established and communicated
- ☐ Consistent application of policies across all employees
- ☐ Progressive discipline follows established procedures
- ☐ Documentation focuses on job-related impacts and behaviors
- ☐ Accommodation considerations integrated into performance plans

Crisis Response:

- ☐ Safety assessment protocols established and followed
- ☐ Emergency contact information readily available
- ☐ Professional resources identified and accessible
- ☐ Legal counsel consultation procedures defined
- ☐ Confidentiality requirements understood and maintained

Documentation Templates

Incident Documentation Template:

```
Date: _____
Time: _____
Location: _____
Individuals Present: _____

Objective Description of Incident:
[Record specific behaviors, statements, and actions
observed. Use factual language without interpretation or
judgment.]

Impact on Work Environment:
[Describe specific effects on productivity, safety, or
team functioning.]

Immediate Actions Taken:
[List steps taken to address the situation.]
```

Follow-up Required:
[Identify next steps and timeline.]

Prepared by: _____
Date: _____

Accommodation Request Documentation:

Employee Name: _____
Position: _____
Date of Request: _____

Nature of Request:
[Describe specific accommodation being requested.]

Medical Documentation Provided:
[Summarize medical information relevant to accommodation.]

Essential Job Functions Analysis:
[List core job requirements and relationship to requested accommodation.]

Accommodation Options Considered:
[Document all options explored and rationale for decisions.]

Implementation Plan:
[Detail specific accommodations approved and implementation timeline.]

Review Schedule:
[Establish dates for effectiveness evaluation.]

Appendix B: Assessment Tools and Worksheets

Team Health Assessment

This comprehensive evaluation tool helps managers and team leaders assess the overall functioning and well-being of their teams, particularly in environments where personality disorders may be present.

Team Communication Assessment:

- Rate team members' ability to express ideas openly (1-10 scale)
- Evaluate frequency of misunderstandings or communication breakdowns
- Assess whether all voices are heard during team discussions
- Measure comfort level with providing and receiving feedback
- Analyze conflict resolution effectiveness

Interpersonal Relationship Quality:

- Document patterns of collaboration versus competition
- Identify alliance formations or clique development
- Assess trust levels between team members
- Evaluate mutual support and assistance patterns
- Monitor for signs of isolation or exclusion

Productivity and Performance Indicators:

- Track project completion rates and timeline adherence
- Measure quality of collaborative work products
- Assess individual versus team achievement patterns
- Monitor absenteeism and turnover trends
- Evaluate customer or stakeholder satisfaction with team output

Stress and Well-being Factors:

- Assess overall team morale and job satisfaction
- Identify sources of team stress and tension
- Evaluate work-life balance indicators
- Monitor use of employee assistance resources
- Track sick leave and stress-related absences

Personal Stress and Impact Tracker

This self-assessment tool helps individuals monitor their own well-being and identify when personality disorder impacts from colleagues are affecting their health and job performance.

Physical Stress Indicators:

- Sleep quality and duration changes
- Appetite or eating pattern modifications
- Headaches, muscle tension, or other physical symptoms
- Energy level fluctuations
- Illness frequency or duration changes

Emotional Well-being Measures:

- Mood stability and emotional regulation
- Anxiety or worry levels about work
- Feelings of frustration or anger frequency
- Sense of accomplishment and job satisfaction
- Confidence and self-esteem at work

Professional Performance Impact:

- Productivity and quality of work output
- Ability to concentrate and focus
- Creativity and problem-solving effectiveness
- Relationship quality with colleagues and clients
- Career motivation and goal pursuit

Behavioral Change Indicators:

- Social interaction patterns at work
- Participation in team activities and meetings
- Help-seeking or isolation behaviors
- Conflict avoidance or confrontation patterns
- Work schedule or routine modifications

Stay-or-Go Decision Matrix

This decision-making framework helps individuals systematically evaluate their workplace situation and make informed choices about remaining in challenging environments or seeking alternatives.

Situation Assessment (Rate 1-10):

- Frequency of personality disorder incidents affecting you
- Severity of impacts on your work performance
- Organizational response to reported problems
- Available support resources and their effectiveness
- Your ability to implement protective strategies

Personal Threshold Analysis:

- Financial flexibility and security considerations
- Career advancement opportunities in current position
- Impact on family and personal relationships
- Health effects (physical and mental)
- Professional development and skill building potential

Options Evaluation:

- Internal transfer possibilities within organization
- External job market conditions and opportunities
- Professional development alternatives
- Legal protection or intervention options
- Support resources that might improve current situation

Implementation Planning:

- Timeline for chosen course of action
- Resource requirements and preparation needed
- Risk mitigation strategies
- Success indicators and measurement methods
- Contingency plans for unexpected developments

Boundary Setting Worksheet

This practical tool helps individuals identify, establish, and maintain professional boundaries when working with personality-disordered colleagues.

Boundary Identification:

- What behaviors from others make you uncomfortable?
- Which of your personal/professional information needs protection?
- What types of requests or demands will you not accept?
- How much time and energy can you reasonably give to others' problems?
- What physical space and environmental needs do you have?

Boundary Communication:

- How will you clearly state your limits?
- What specific language will you use to enforce boundaries?
- How will you remain professional while maintaining limits?
- What responses will you prepare for boundary testing?
- How will you handle emotional manipulation or guilt trips?

Boundary Maintenance:

- What support systems will help you maintain boundaries?
- How will you monitor your own boundary compliance?
- What strategies will you use when feeling guilty about limits?
- How will you handle escalation when boundaries are challenged?

- What self-care practices will support your boundary maintenance?

Manager's Observation Log

This systematic documentation tool helps managers track behavioral patterns and workplace impacts while maintaining objectivity and legal compliance.

Behavioral Observation Record:

```
Date: _____
Time: _____
Setting: _____
Individuals Present: _____

Specific Behaviors Observed:
[Record exact actions, statements, and interactions
without interpretation]

Duration and Frequency:
[Note how long behaviors lasted and how often they
occur]

Triggering Events or Context:
[Identify what preceded the observed behaviors]

Impact on Others:
[Document specific effects on colleagues, clients, or
work environment]

Follow-up Actions Needed:
[Identify next steps for addressing observations]
```

Appendix C: Resources and Professional Contacts

National Mental Health Organizations

National Alliance on Mental Illness (NAMI)

- Website: www.nami.org
- Phone: 1-800-950-NAMI (6264)
- Services: Education, support groups, advocacy, resource referrals
- Workplace programs: Mental health awareness training, stigma reduction initiatives

Mental Health America

- Website: www.mhanational.org
- Phone: 1-800-969-6642
- Services: Screening tools, educational resources, policy advocacy
- Workplace focus: Employee mental health promotion, stress management resources

National Institute of Mental Health (NIMH)

- Website: www.nimh.nih.gov
- Services: Research information, educational materials, treatment guidelines
- Resources: Fact sheets on personality disorders, workplace mental health research

American Psychological Association (APA)

- Website: www.apa.org
- Services: Professional referrals, educational resources, research publications

- Workplace programs: Consultation services, training materials, best practices guides

Legal Resources

U.S. Equal Employment Opportunity Commission (EEOC)

- Website: www.eeoc.gov
- Phone: 1-800-669-4000
- Services: Discrimination complaint processing, legal guidance, employer education
- Resources: ADA compliance materials, mental health accommodation guidelines

U.S. Department of Labor - Office of Disability Employment Policy

- Website: www.dol.gov/agencies/odep
- Services: Accommodation guidance, employer resources, policy development
- Programs: Job Accommodation Network (JAN), disability employment initiatives

State Civil Rights Agencies

- Services vary by state: discrimination complaint processing, mediation services, legal enforcement
- Resources: State-specific employment law guidance, accommodation requirements

Employment Law Attorneys

- Services: Legal consultation, representation, policy review
- Specializations: ADA compliance, wrongful termination, accommodation disputes

Professional Associations

Society for Human Resource Management (SHRM)

- Website: www.shrm.org
- Services: Professional development, certification programs, legal updates
- Resources: Mental health toolkit, accommodation guidance, best practices

International Association of Business Communicators (IABC)

- Website: www.iabc.com
- Services: Communication training, professional development, networking
- Focus: Crisis communication, internal communications, change management

Association of Workplace Investigators (AWI)

- Website: www.awi.org
- Services: Training, certification, professional standards
- Expertise: Workplace investigations, harassment claims, documentation practices

National Association of Social Workers (NASW)

- Website: www.socialworkers.org
- Services: Professional referrals, ethical guidelines, continuing education
- Workplace focus: Employee assistance programs, mental health consultation

Recommended Training Programs

Traliant

- Website: www.traliant.com
- Offerings: Managing difficult employees, harassment prevention, mental health awareness

- Format: Online interactive training, customizable content, compliance tracking

ClickSafety

- Website: www.clicksafety.com
- Offerings: Workplace safety, crisis management, emergency response
- Format: Online courses, certification programs, mobile learning

Mental Health First Aid

- Website: www.mentalhealthfirstaid.org
- Offerings: Crisis intervention training, mental health awareness, early intervention
- Format: Instructor-led training, certification programs, ongoing support

Crisis & Trauma Resource Institute

- Website: www.ctrinstitute.com
- Offerings: De-escalation training, trauma-informed care, crisis intervention
- Format: Workshops, online learning, train-the-trainer programs

Crisis Hotlines and Emergency Resources

National Suicide Prevention Lifeline

- Phone: 988
- Available: 24/7/365
- Services: Crisis intervention, suicide prevention, emotional support

Crisis Text Line

- Text: HOME to 741741
- Available: 24/7/365
- Services: Text-based crisis support, trained crisis counselors

SAMHSA National Helpline

- Phone: 1-800-662-HELP (4357)
- Available: 24/7/365
- Services: Treatment referrals, information services, local resource referrals

National Domestic Violence Hotline

- Phone: 1-800-799-7233
- Available: 24/7/365
- Services: Crisis intervention, safety planning, resource referrals

Appendix D: Sample Policies and Procedures

Accommodation Request Process

Purpose: To establish clear procedures for requesting and evaluating reasonable accommodations for employees with mental health conditions while maintaining compliance with applicable laws.

Policy Statement: [Organization name] is committed to providing equal employment opportunities and reasonable accommodations for qualified individuals with disabilities, including mental health conditions. This policy outlines the process for requesting, evaluating, and implementing workplace accommodations.

Procedure:

1. **Initial Request**
    - Employee submits written request to HR or immediate supervisor
    - Request should include general nature of accommodation needed
    - No medical diagnosis required at initial request stage
    - HR initiates interactive process within 5 business days
2. **Medical Documentation**
    - HR provides medical inquiry form to employee's healthcare provider
    - Documentation must establish disability and functional limitations
    - Medical information remains confidential and stored separately
    - Additional documentation may be requested if initial submission insufficient
3. **Job Analysis and Accommodation Assessment**
    - HR conducts analysis of essential job functions
    - Identifies potential reasonable accommodations
    - Considers undue hardship factors

- 4. **Decision and Implementation**
    - o Consults with employee, supervisor, and legal counsel as needed
    - o HR provides written decision within 15 business days of complete documentation
    - o If approved, implementation timeline established
    - o If denied, specific reasons provided with appeal rights
    - o Accommodation effectiveness reviewed every 6 months

Progressive Discipline Policy Template

Purpose: To provide fair, consistent, and legally compliant approach to addressing performance and behavioral issues while considering accommodation needs for employees with mental health conditions.

Policy Framework:

Step 1: Informal Coaching

- Immediate supervisor addresses minor issues through coaching conversation
- Documentation includes date, specific behaviors, expectations clarified
- Employee acknowledgment obtained but formal disciplinary record not created
- Accommodation needs assessed if mental health factors apparent

Step 2: Verbal Warning

- Formal verbal warning for continued problems or more serious issues
- Written documentation placed in personnel file
- Clear expectations and improvement timeline established
- Accommodation discussion initiated if not previously conducted

Step 3: Written Warning

- Formal written warning for continued non-compliance
- Specific improvement plan with measurable objectives
- Timeline for improvement typically 30-60 days
- Accommodation implementation or modification considered

Step 4: Final Written Warning

- Last chance before termination consideration
- Clear statement that termination may result from continued problems
- Accommodation effectiveness evaluated and modified if necessary
- Legal review conducted before issuance

Step 5: Termination

- Only after all previous steps completed (except for gross misconduct)
- Legal and accommodation compliance verified
- Documentation review confirms appropriate process followed
- Exit procedures include final accommodation discussion

Workplace Behavior Standards

Professional Communication Requirements:

- Treat all colleagues with respect and courtesy
- Use appropriate language and tone in all interactions
- Listen actively and respond constructively to feedback
- Address conflicts directly with involved parties when appropriate
- Maintain confidentiality of sensitive information

Teamwork and Collaboration Expectations:

- Participate constructively in team meetings and activities

- Share credit for collaborative achievements
- Offer assistance to colleagues when appropriate
- Accept responsibility for individual contributions to team problems
- Support team decisions once made through proper process

Emotional Regulation Standards:

- Maintain professional demeanor during stressful situations
- Seek appropriate support for personal problems affecting work
- Take breaks as needed to manage emotional states
- Avoid letting personal emotions negatively impact colleagues
- Use employee assistance resources when struggling with emotional issues

Boundary and Respect Requirements:

- Respect colleagues' personal space and privacy
- Limit personal discussions to appropriate times and settings
- Avoid gossip or inappropriate sharing of personal information
- Maintain professional relationships with appropriate boundaries
- Report concerns about boundary violations to supervision or HR

Crisis Response Procedures

Level 1: Early Warning Response

- Supervisor consultation with HR within 24 hours
- Documentation of concerning behaviors or statements
- Employee assistance program referral offered
- Informal support and accommodation discussion
- Close monitoring and follow-up scheduled

Level 2: Urgent Intervention

- Immediate supervisor and HR involvement

- Safety assessment conducted
- EAP crisis consultation initiated
- Possible modification of work assignments
- Enhanced support and monitoring implemented

Level 3: Emergency Response

- Immediate safety assessment and protection measures
- Emergency mental health consultation obtained
- Law enforcement contacted if safety threats present
- Crisis team activation
- Family notification considered with employee consent

Level 4: Critical Incident

- Emergency services contacted immediately
- Workplace security measures implemented
- Crisis team and leadership notification
- Media and communication management
- Post-incident support and debriefing planned

Return-to-Work Guidelines

Pre-Return Assessment:

- Medical clearance from treating healthcare provider
- Fitness for duty evaluation if required
- Accommodation needs assessment
- Safety and readiness evaluation
- Support system planning

Gradual Reintegration Process:

- Phased return with modified schedule or duties
- Regular check-ins with supervisor and HR
- Ongoing accommodation effectiveness monitoring
- Adjustment of support as needed
- Documentation of progress and challenges

Support System Activation:

- Employee assistance program continuation
- Supervisory training on supporting returning employee
- Team preparation and communication
- External treatment coordination
- Ongoing monitoring and adjustment

Appendix E: Case Studies and Scenarios

NPD in Leadership: A Tech Startup Story

Background: TechVenture, a rapidly growing software startup, hired Marcus Chen as Chief Technology Officer based on his impressive technical background and confident leadership presence. The CEO, Sarah Williams, was attracted to Marcus's vision and apparent ability to drive innovation in their competitive market.

Initial Success: During his first six months, Marcus appeared to deliver exceptional results. He redesigned the development process, hired several senior engineers, and presented compelling technical roadmaps to investors. His confidence in client meetings helped secure major contracts, and his team seemed to respect his technical expertise.

Emerging Problems: By month eight, concerning patterns began emerging. Team members started reporting that Marcus took credit for their innovative solutions while blaming them for any implementation problems. He dominated technical discussions, dismissed others' ideas without consideration, and showed no empathy when colleagues faced personal challenges. His expectations for recognition seemed excessive—he expected special parking, a larger office, and exemptions from company policies that applied to other executives.

Crisis Development: The situation escalated when Marcus began undermining other executives to position himself as indispensable. He shared confidential technical information with investors to gain their support against his colleagues. When the CEO provided feedback about his interpersonal style, Marcus responded with rage, accusing her of being incompetent and threatening to leave and take key clients with him. His behavior created a toxic environment where team members were afraid to innovate or speak up about problems.

Resolution Attempts: Sarah attempted various interventions including executive coaching, clear boundary setting, and team restructuring. However, Marcus viewed these efforts as attacks on his competence and became increasingly hostile. His narcissistic patterns proved resistant to feedback and accommodation. When he began creating legal risks through inappropriate client communications and team harassment, the board made the difficult decision to terminate his employment.

Lessons Learned:

- Narcissistic traits that appear as confidence during interviews can become destructive in leadership roles
- Early intervention and clear boundaries are essential before patterns become entrenched
- Technical competence cannot compensate for interpersonal dysfunction in leadership positions
- Board and CEO support is necessary for addressing executive-level personality disorder issues

BPD in Healthcare: Managing Emotional Volatility

Background: Jennifer Martinez, a registered nurse with five years of experience, joined the emergency department at Regional Medical Center during a staffing shortage. Her clinical skills were excellent, and she initially seemed enthusiastic about the fast-paced emergency environment.

Initial Adjustment: Jennifer quickly developed intense relationships with several colleagues, spending hours after shifts providing emotional support and sharing personal struggles. She seemed dedicated to patient care and volunteered for extra shifts. However, her emotional reactions to routine feedback seemed disproportionate, and she often became tearful when discussing minor work issues.

Escalating Patterns: Within three months, Jennifer's emotional volatility began affecting patient care. She would idealize certain doctors as "amazing" then shift to viewing them as "incompetent" after minor disagreements. Her relationships with colleagues followed similar patterns—intense friendships that suddenly became bitter conflicts. She began having emotional outbursts during shift changes, creating tension that affected the entire department.

Critical Incident: The situation reached crisis level when Jennifer threatened suicide after a supervisor provided routine feedback about documentation procedures. She interpreted the feedback as rejection and abandonment, despite reassurances about her job security. The incident required emergency mental health intervention and raised serious concerns about patient safety and team stability.

Intervention Strategy: Nurse Manager Patricia developed a comprehensive support plan that included:

- Clear, written communication about expectations and feedback
- Structured supervision with consistent scheduling
- Modified assignments that provided stability while maintaining challenge
- Connection with employee assistance program for ongoing support
- Team education about supporting colleagues with mental health challenges

Accommodation Implementation: Jennifer's accommodations included:

- Private space for emotional regulation breaks
- Written summaries of all feedback and evaluations
- Flexible scheduling to accommodate therapy appointments
- Modified conflict resolution procedures that prevented escalation
- Ongoing check-ins with EAP counselor

Positive Outcomes: With appropriate support and accommodation, Jennifer's performance improved significantly. Her emotional volatility decreased, patient care quality remained high, and team relationships stabilized. The department learned valuable lessons about early intervention and the importance of mental health support in high-stress healthcare environments.

Key Success Factors:

- Early recognition of borderline patterns and prompt intervention
- Comprehensive accommodation planning that addressed specific triggers
- Team education and support for managing complex interpersonal dynamics
- Ongoing professional mental health support and monitoring
- Leadership commitment to balancing individual needs with patient safety

OCPD in Finance: When Perfectionism Paralyzes

Background: Robert Thompson, a senior financial analyst with impeccable credentials and attention to detail, joined Pinnacle Investment Management to lead their risk assessment team. His previous employers praised his thoroughness and analytical capabilities, making him seem like an ideal fit for the detail-oriented financial environment.

Initial Performance: Robert's work quality was exceptional—his financial models were incredibly detailed, his reports were thoroughly researched, and he caught errors that others missed. Senior management appreciated his meticulous approach and began assigning him increasingly complex projects. His dedication was evident as he regularly worked evenings and weekends to ensure perfection.

Emerging Challenges: Problems became apparent when project timelines began extending far beyond reasonable expectations. Robert would spend days perfecting minor details while missing major deadlines. He couldn't delegate effectively because others didn't meet his impossible standards, creating bottlenecks that affected the entire team. His insistence on reviewing every document multiple times delayed critical investment decisions.

Team Impact: Robert's perfectionism began affecting his colleagues' productivity and morale. He would revise collaborative documents endlessly, becoming frustrated when others suggested that "good enough" might be sufficient for certain tasks. Team members started avoiding projects that involved Robert because they knew the work would be held to impossible standards and timelines would be unrealistic.

Performance Crisis: The situation reached a breaking point when Robert's perfectionist paralysis caused the firm to miss a critical investment opportunity. His analysis was months overdue because he insisted on collecting additional data and refining his models beyond any practical necessity. The lost opportunity cost the firm millions in potential revenue and damaged client relationships.

Management Response: Department Director Lisa Chen implemented a structured approach to managing Robert's OCPD traits:

- Clear deadlines with interim checkpoints to prevent perfectionist delays
- Collaborative decision-making about when analyses were "sufficient"
- Modified assignments that leveraged his detail orientation without paralyzing timelines
- Training on delegation and collaborative work styles
- Regular supervision focused on balancing quality with efficiency

Accommodation Strategies:

- Extended deadlines for complex projects with interim deliverable requirements
- Partnership with colleagues who provided "good enough" reality checks

- Training on project management and prioritization techniques
- Modified performance metrics that balanced quality with timeliness
- Stress management resources to address perfectionist anxiety

Resolution: With appropriate structure and support, Robert learned to channel his perfectionist tendencies productively. He became the team's quality control specialist while others handled time-sensitive preliminary analyses. His attention to detail remained valuable while no longer paralyzing team productivity.

ASPD in Sales: Ethics and Boundaries

Background: David Rodriguez joined Global Solutions Corporation as a senior sales representative with an impressive track record of exceeding targets at previous companies. His charm, confidence, and apparent ability to close difficult deals made him an attractive hire during a competitive period.

Early Success: David immediately began generating impressive sales numbers, securing contracts that other representatives had been unable to close. His clients seemed to appreciate his confidence and responsiveness. He quickly became one of the top performers and was considered for promotion to sales management.

Red Flags Emerge: Within six months, concerning patterns became apparent to observant colleagues. David's expense reports included questionable items, he made promises to clients that the company couldn't fulfill, and he shared confidential pricing information inappropriately. When questioned about these issues, he provided plausible explanations that deflected responsibility.

Escalating Problems: David's antisocial traits became more obvious as he manipulated client information to steal prospects from colleagues, falsified activity reports to inflate his performance metrics, and violated confidentiality agreements by sharing sensitive competitive information. He showed no remorse when confronted about these behaviors, instead becoming defensive and blaming company policies or colleague incompetence.

Crisis Point: The situation became untenable when several major clients complained about David's deceptive practices. He had promised services the company didn't provide, misrepresented pricing structures, and created contractual obligations that were financially impossible to fulfill. His behavior threatened long-term client relationships and created significant legal liability for the organization.

Management Challenges: Sales Manager Karen White faced difficult decisions about how to address David's behavior:

- His sales numbers were excellent, creating pressure to overlook ethical concerns
- His manipulation made it difficult to gather clear evidence of policy violations
- He was skilled at deflecting blame and creating doubt about accusations
- Traditional coaching and feedback approaches proved completely ineffective

Intervention Attempts: Various strategies were attempted:

- Clear documentation of policy violations and expected behaviors
- Enhanced supervision and monitoring of client interactions
- Ethics training and boundary setting
- Progressive discipline with explicit consequences
- Legal consultation about evidence gathering and termination procedures

Resolution: Despite intervention efforts, David's antisocial patterns persisted and escalated. When he began making threats against colleagues who reported his misconduct and engaging in behaviors that created safety concerns, the organization terminated his employment. The decision was supported by extensive documentation and legal consultation, but the company faced months of client relationship repair and legal risk management.

Organizational Learning:

- Enhanced background checking procedures to identify patterns of ethical violations
- Improved interview techniques to assess character and integrity
- Modified sales metrics to include ethical behavior and long-term relationship building
- Enhanced training for managers on recognizing and addressing antisocial behavior patterns

Team Recovery After Toxic Departure

Background: The marketing department at Creative Communications had endured eighteen months of disruption caused by Patricia Lawson, whose histrionic personality traits had created ongoing interpersonal drama and productivity challenges. After Patricia's eventual departure, the team faced the complex task of rebuilding trust, restoring collaborative relationships, and recovering their professional effectiveness.

Damage Assessment: Department Director Michael Chen conducted a thorough evaluation of the team's condition following Patricia's departure:

- Team members had developed defensive communication patterns and were reluctant to share ideas
- Productivity had declined by approximately 30% due to energy spent managing interpersonal drama
- Several talented employees had requested transfers or were considering leaving
- Client relationships had been affected by inconsistent service and internal conflicts
- Team morale was low, with high stress levels and reduced job satisfaction

Immediate Stabilization: Michael's first priority was stabilizing the team and preventing further deterioration:

- Individual meetings with each team member to assess their experience and concerns
- Team meeting to acknowledge the challenges and commit to positive change
- Clear communication that the problematic behaviors were not acceptable and would not be tolerated
- Reassurance about job security and organizational commitment to team success
- Connection with employee assistance resources for those needing additional support

Relationship Repair Process: Rebuilding professional relationships required systematic attention:

- Facilitated team discussions about communication preferences and working styles
- Collaborative development of new team norms and behavioral expectations
- Conflict resolution training for all team members
- Team-building activities focused on professional collaboration rather than personal sharing
- Regular check-ins to monitor relationship quality and address emerging issues

Process and System Recovery: Many work processes had been modified to accommodate Patricia's dramatic tendencies and needed restoration:

- Elimination of excessive documentation and approval procedures that had been implemented for protection
- Restoration of normal meeting formats and decision-making processes
- Reestablishment of collaborative project management approaches

- Removal of formal communication protocols that were no longer necessary
- Return to standard feedback and performance evaluation procedures

Skill Development and Training: Team members needed skill development to function effectively in healthier environment:

- Communication skills training focused on direct, professional interaction
- Conflict resolution skills for addressing disagreements constructively
- Collaboration techniques for effective teamwork
- Stress management and resilience building
- Professional development opportunities that had been delayed during the crisis period

Culture Restoration: Rebuilding positive team culture required intentional effort:

- Reestablishment of team traditions and social activities
- Recognition and celebration of professional achievements
- Encouragement of innovation and creative risk-taking
- Development of shared goals and vision for team success
- Creation of psychological safety for authentic professional expression

Success Monitoring: Michael tracked recovery progress through multiple indicators:

- Productivity metrics showing gradual improvement to pre-crisis levels
- Team satisfaction surveys indicating improved morale and job satisfaction
- Client feedback showing restored service quality and relationship stability
- Retention rates demonstrating reduced turnover intentions

- Innovation measures indicating renewed creative output and idea generation

Long-term Prevention: The team developed strategies to prevent similar problems in the future:

- Enhanced interview and reference checking procedures
- Early intervention protocols for addressing interpersonal problems
- Regular team health assessments and culture monitoring
- Training for all team members on maintaining healthy professional boundaries
- Clear policies and procedures for addressing disruptive behavior patterns

Positive Outcomes: Within twelve months, the marketing department had not only recovered but achieved higher performance levels than before the crisis:

- Productivity exceeded pre-crisis levels by 15%
- Team satisfaction scores reached all-time highs
- Client relationships were stronger due to improved collaboration and service consistency
- Employee retention improved significantly
- The team's reputation within the organization was restored and enhanced

Key Success Factors:

- Leadership commitment to systematic recovery rather than hoping problems would resolve naturally
- Individual attention to each team member's experience and needs
- Systematic address of both interpersonal and procedural issues
- Investment in skill development and training
- Long-term perspective focused on prevention as well as recovery
- Recognition that recovery takes time and sustained effort

Reference

American Psychiatric Association. (2022). *Diagnostic and Statistical Manual of Mental Disorders, Fifth Edition, Text Revision (DSM-5-TR)*. American Psychiatric Publishing.

Annual Reviews. (2024). Mental Health in the Workplace. Retrieved from https://www.annualreviews.org/content/journals/10.1146/annurev-orgpsych-120920-050527

Assess Candidates. (2025). Workplace Personality Tests for Hiring | 2025 Guide. Retrieved from https://www.assesscandidates.com/personality-assessment-questionnaire-for-recruitment/

ADA National Network. (2024). Mental Health Conditions in the Workplace and the ADA. Retrieved from https://adata.org/factsheet/health

Cleveland Clinic. (2024). DSM-5: What It Is & What It Diagnoses. Retrieved from https://my.clevelandclinic.org/health/articles/24291-diagnostic-and-statistical-manual-dsm-5

Comcare. (2024). Intervene early. Retrieved from https://www.comcare.gov.au/safe-healthy-work/healthy-workplace/intervene-early

U.S. Department of Labor. (2024). Accommodations for Employees with Mental Health Conditions. Retrieved from https://www.dol.gov/agencies/odep/program-areas/mental-health/maximizing-productivity-accommodations-for-employees-with-psychiatric-disabilities

U.S. Equal Employment Opportunity Commission. (2024). Depression, PTSD, & Other Mental Health Conditions in the Workplace: Your Legal Rights. Retrieved from https://www.eeoc.gov/laws/guidance/depression-ptsd-other-mental-health-conditions-workplace-your-legal-rights

U.S. Equal Employment Opportunity Commission. (2024). Enforcement Guidance on the ADA and Psychiatric Disabilities. Retrieved from https://www.eeoc.gov/laws/guidance/enforcement-guidance-ada-and-psychiatric-disabilities

U.S. Equal Employment Opportunity Commission. (2024). EEOC Issues Publication on the Rights of Job Applicants and Employees with Mental Health Conditions. Retrieved from https://www.eeoc.gov/newsroom/eeoc-issues-publication-rights-job-applicants-and-employees-mental-health-conditions

U.S. Equal Employment Opportunity Commission. (2024). Mental Health Conditions: Resources for Job Seekers, Employees, and Employers. Retrieved from https://www.eeoc.gov/mental-health-conditions-resources-job-seekers-employees-and-employers

Borderline in the ACT. (2024). BPD in the workplace. Retrieved from https://www.borderlineintheact.org.au/family-friends-and-carers/relationships/bpd-in-the-workplace/

Forensic Psychiatry Now. (2024). Psychiatric Fitness for Duty and Occupational Assessment. Retrieved from https://forensicpsychiatrynow.com/fitness-for-duty-and-job-assessment/

Dr. Lisa Long. (2024). Fitness For Duty Evaluation Guide | Infographic. Retrieved from https://www.drlisalong.com/blog/psychological-fitness-for-duty-evaluations-ffde-guide-service

Job Accommodation Network (JAN). (2024). Personality Disorder. Retrieved from https://askjan.org/disabilities/Personality-Disorder.cfm

Managed Healthcare Executive. (2024). Personality Disorders in the Workplace: The Impulsive, Divisive Employee. Retrieved from https://www.managedhealthcareexecutive.com/view/personality-disorders-workplace-impulsive-divisive-employee

Mental Health America. (2024). Understanding Personality Disorders in the DSM-5. Retrieved from https://www.mentalhealth.com/library/dsm-5-personality-disorders

National Center for Biotechnology Information. (2024). Does Having a Dysfunctional Personality Hurt Your Career? Axis II Personality Disorders and Labor Market Outcomes. PMC. Retrieved from https://www.ncbi.nlm.nih.gov/pmc/articles/PMC3204880/

National Center for Biotechnology Information. (2024). Fitness for Duty and Return to Work - StatPearls. Retrieved from https://www.ncbi.nlm.nih.gov/sites/books/NBK610688/

National Center for Biotechnology Information. (2024). Insights into workplace bullying: psychosocial drivers and effective interventions - PMC. Retrieved from https://www.ncbi.nlm.nih.gov/pmc/articles/PMC4924877/

National Center for Biotechnology Information. (2024). Narcissistic Personality Disorder - StatPearls. Retrieved from https://www.ncbi.nlm.nih.gov/books/NBK556001/

National Center for Biotechnology Information. (2024). Persisting Menace: A Case-Based Study of Remote Workplace Bullying in India - PMC. Retrieved from https://www.ncbi.nlm.nih.gov/pmc/articles/PMC9761046/

National Center for Biotechnology Information. (2024). Personality Disorder - StatPearls. Retrieved from https://www.ncbi.nlm.nih.gov/books/NBK556058/

National Center for Biotechnology Information. (2024). Personality Dysfunction and Employment Dysfunction: Double, Double, Toil and

Trouble. PMC. Retrieved from
https://www.ncbi.nlm.nih.gov/pmc/articles/PMC2861520/

Office of Personnel Management. (2024). What is an Employee Assistance Program (EAP)? Retrieved from https://www.opm.gov/frequently-asked-questions/work-life-faq/employee-assistance-program-eap/what-is-an-employee-assistance-program-eap/

Oxford Academic. (2014). Personality disorders in the workplace. *Occupational Medicine*, 64(8), 566-574. Retrieved from https://academic.oup.com/occmed/article/64/8/566/1429812

Psych Central. (2024). Cluster B Personality Disorders: Types, Symptoms, and Treatment. Retrieved from https://psychcentral.com/disorders/cluster-b-personality-disorders

Psych Central. (2024). Histrionic Personality Disorder in the Workplace: Signs and Symptoms. Retrieved from https://psychcentral.com/lib/characteristics-of-a-histrionic-pd-in-a-work-environment

Psych Central. (2024). The Grey Rock Method: A Technique for Handling Toxic Behavior. Retrieved from https://psychcentral.com/health/grey-rock-method

Psych Eval Expert. (2024). Navigating the Process: How to Obtain Psychological Testing for Fitness for Duty. Retrieved from https://psychevalexpert.com/evaluation/navigating-the-process-how-to-obtain-psychological-testing-for-fitness-for-duty/

Psychology 360. (2024). Fitness for Duty & Return to Work. Retrieved from https://psyc360.com/fitness-for-duty-return-to-work/

Psychology Today. (2024). Navigating Borderline Personality Disorder in the Workplace. Retrieved from https://www.psychologytoday.com/us/blog/the-discomfort-zone/202402/navigating-borderline-personality-disorder-in-the-workplace

PubMed. (2015). Workplace interventions for common mental disorders: a systematic meta-review. Retrieved from https://pubmed.ncbi.nlm.nih.gov/26620157/

PubMed. (2024). Psychiatric fitness-for-duty evaluations. Retrieved from https://pubmed.ncbi.nlm.nih.gov/16904505/

PubMed. (2023). Examining generational differences as a moderator of extreme-context perception and its impact on work alienation organizational outcomes: Implications for the workplace and remote work transformation. Retrieved from https://pubmed.ncbi.nlm.nih.gov/37596807/

PubMed Central. (2019). Barriers and facilitators to employment in borderline personality disorder: A qualitative study among patients, mental health practitioners and insurance physicians. Retrieved from https://pmc.ncbi.nlm.nih.gov/articles/PMC6650068/

PubMed Central. (2019). Interventions for prevention of bullying in the workplace - PMC. Retrieved from https://pmc.ncbi.nlm.nih.gov/articles/PMC6464940/

Spring Health. (2024). How to Equip Employees with Borderline Personality Disorder to Flourish. Retrieved from https://www.springhealth.com/blog/how-to-equip-employees-with-borderline-personality-disorder-to-flourish

USC Policy. (2024). Fitness-for-Duty Evaluation - Policies and Policy Governance. Retrieved from https://policy.usc.edu/fitness-for-duty-evaluation/

Workplace Mental Health. (2024). Early warning signs of mental health problems at work. Retrieved from https://returntowork.workplace-mentalhealth.net.au/early-warning-signs-of-mental-health-problems-at-work/

Workplace Mental Health. (2024). Employee Assistance Programs. Retrieved from https://workplacementalhealth.org/mental-health-topics/employee-assistance-programs

Workplace Mental Health. (2024). Reasonable Job Accommodations. Retrieved from https://workplacementalhealth.org/mental-health-topics/reasonable-job-accommodations

Zephyr Care Mental Health. (2024). What to Expect from a Pre-Employment Fitness for Duty Psychological Evaluation. Retrieved from https://zephyrcare.com/blog/what-to-expect-from-a-pre-employment-fitness-for-duty-psychological-evaluation

BetterUp. (2024). What Is Gaslighting at Work? 6 Signs of Gaslighting and How to Deal. Retrieved from https://www.betterup.com/blog/gaslighting-at-work

Business Pathways. (2024). Managing Different Personalities in the Workplace. Retrieved from https://www.business-pathways.com/blog/posts/managing-different-personalities-workplace

Center for Creative Leadership. (2024). How Leaders Can Build Psychological Safety at Work. Retrieved from https://www.ccl.org/articles/leading-effectively-articles/what-is-psychological-safety-at-work/

ClickSafety. (2024). How to Manage a Difficult Employee - Course. Retrieved from https://www.clicksafety.com/managing-difficult-employees

David Burkus. (2025). Managing Generations At Work: The Differences Don't Really Make A Difference. Retrieved from https://davidburkus.com/2025/03/managing-generations-at-work/

Defuse - De-Escalation Training. (2024). De-Escalation Techniques: 4 Effective Strategies for All Industries. Retrieved from https://deescalation-training.com/2024/05/de-escalation-techniques/

Employee Benefit News. (2024). For younger generations, a toxic workplace is a dealbreaker. Retrieved from https://www.benefitnews.com/news/for-younger-generations-a-toxic-workplace-is-a-dealbreaker

Freshworks. (2024). Freshworks 2024 Global AI Workplace Report. Retrieved from https://www.freshworks.com/resources/reports/workplace-tech/

Gallup. (2024). How to Create a Culture of Psychological Safety. Retrieved from https://www.gallup.com/workplace/236198/create-culture-psychological-safety.aspx

Harvard Business Review. (2019). Generational Differences at Work Are Small. Thinking They're Big Affects Our Behavior. Retrieved from https://hbr.org/2019/08/generational-differences-at-work-are-small-thinking-theyre-big-affects-our-behavior

Harvard Business Review. (2019). How to Manage a Stubborn, Defensive, or Defiant Employee. Retrieved from https://hbr.org/2019/11/how-to-manage-a-stubborn-defensive-or-defiant-employee

Hunt Scanlon Media. (2024). Psychological Safety; The Bedrock of Organizational Culture. Retrieved from https://huntscanlon.com/psychological-safety-the-bedrock-of-organizational-culture/

Intoo. (2024). 13 Essential Manager Training Topics to Learn. Retrieved from https://www.intoo.com/us/blog/manager-training-topics/

LinkedIn. (2024). Workplace Mental Health Early Intervention Strategies. Retrieved from https://www.linkedin.com/pulse/workplace-mental-health-early-intervention-strategies-ally-kelly

Littler. (2024). EEOC Issues Guidance on Mental Health Conditions in the Workplace. Retrieved from https://www.littler.com/publication-press/publication/eeoc-issues-guidance-mental-health-conditions-workplace

McKinsey & Company. (2024). Superagency in the workplace: Empowering people to unlock AI's full potential. Retrieved from https://www.mckinsey.com/capabilities/mckinsey-digital/our-insights/superagency-in-the-workplace-empowering-people-to-unlock-ais-full-potential-at-work

Nolo. (2024). Requesting Reasonable Accommodation for a Mental Disability. Retrieved from https://www.nolo.com/legal-encyclopedia/requesting-reasonable-accommodation-mental-disability.html

Paychex. (2024). Progressive Discipline Process: What Is It and Why Is It Important? Retrieved from https://www.paychex.com/articles/human-resources/what-is-progressive-discipline-policy

Personnel Today. (2024). How to deal with personality disorders in the workplace. Retrieved from https://www.personneltoday.com/hr/how-to-deal-with-personality-disorders-in-the-workplace/

Pollack Peacebuilding Systems. (2024). 7 De-Escalation Skills Essential for Defusing Conflict. Retrieved from https://pollackpeacebuilding.com/blog/de-escalation-skills/

ResearchGate. (2014). Generational differences in workplace behavior. Retrieved from https://www.researchgate.net/publication/264580977_Generational_differences_in_workplace_behavior

Risely. (2024). The silent manipulation: Exposing workplace gaslighting and its effects. Retrieved from https://www.risely.me/workplace-gaslighting-and-effects/

Sage Journals. (2023). Employment interventions to assist people who experience borderline personality disorder: A scoping review. Retrieved from https://journals.sagepub.com/doi/10.1177/00207640231189424

Shipman & Goodwin LLP. (2024). Beware The Legal Risks Of Personality Tests In Hiring. Retrieved from https://www.shipmangoodwin.com/insights/beware-the-legal-risks-of-personality-tests-in-hiring.html

SkillPath. (2024). Dealing with a Narcissist at Work? Try the "Gray Rock" Approach. Retrieved from https://skillpath.com/blog/dealing-with-narcissist-work-gray-rock-approach

Springer. (2024). Persisting Menace: A Case-Based Study of Remote Workplace Bullying in India | International Journal of Bullying Prevention. Retrieved from https://link.springer.com/article/10.1007/s42380-022-00152-8

Symonds Research. (2024). 7 Essential Skills & Training Topics For Managers that matter. Retrieved from https://symondsresearch.com/training-topics/

The Diversity Movement. (2024). Ultimate Guide to Reversing Your Toxic Culture. Retrieved from https://thediversitymovement.com/ultimate-guide-to-reversing-your-toxic-culture/

Tilson HR. (2024). Pros and Cons of Personality Tests in Hiring Process. Retrieved from https://www.tilsonhr.com/pros-and-cons-of-personality-tests-in-hiring-process/

Traliant. (2024). Managing Difficult Employees Training. Retrieved from https://www.traliant.com/courses/managing-difficult-employees-training/

VantageCircle. (2024). Ways To Build Psychological Safety In The Workplace. Retrieved from https://www.vantagecircle.com/en/blog/psychological-safety/

Workable. (2024). Employee progressive discipline policy template. Retrieved from https://resources.workable.com/progressive-discipline-policy

Workhuman. (2024). Toxic Work Culture: Signs of Unhealthy Work Environment and How to Fix It. Retrieved from https://www.workhuman.com/blog/toxic-work-culture-environment/

WorkLife. (2025). Technology will shape workplace productivity in 2025, but some warn of AI overload. Retrieved from https://www.worklife.news/technology/technology-will-shape-workplace-productivity-in-2025-but-some-warn-of-ai-overload/

Worksmartlivesmart. (2024). Gaslighting in the Workplace: Recognizing and Addressing Psychological Manipulation. Retrieved from https://worksmartlivesmart.com/gaslighting-in-the-workplace/

www.ingramcontent.com/pod-product-compliance
Lightning Source LLC
Chambersburg PA
CBHW071153160426
43196CB00011B/2071